One in Christ™

Student Book

Grade 5

CONCORDIA PUBLISHING HOUSE · SAINT LOUIS

Copyright © 2011 Concordia Publishing House
3558 S. Jefferson Avenue, St. Louis, MO 63118-3968
1-800-325-3040 • www.cph.org

Written by Katie Dennert, Nicole Dreyer, Rebecca Fisher, Jane Fryar, Carol Geisler, Joan Gerber, Diane Grebing, Jeanette Groth, Gretchen Hintz, Glory Jansen, Karen Jensen, Julaine Kammrath, Alaina Kleinbeck, Judy Lillquist, Karen Markin, Aaron Pierce, Eileen Ritter

Edited by Carolyn Bergt

Series editors: Rodney L. Rathmann, Carolyn Bergt, Brenda Trunkhill

Editorial assistant: Amanda G. Lansche

Cover photo: © Duncan Walker/iStockphoto.com

Manufactured in the United States of America, Burlington, WI / 032337 / 409333

4   5   6   7   8   9   10   11   12   13   23   22   21   20   19   18   17   16   15   14

Table of Contents

Unit 1—God and His Word

Unit 2—The Holy Spirit Blesses the Church: The Third Article

Unit 3—God the Father's Gracious Gifts: The First Article

Unit 4—Jesus Brings Salvation: The Second Article

Unit 5—God Hears and Answers His People: The Lord's Prayer

Unit 6—Worship: In Liturgy and In Life

Unit 7—The Sacraments: Holy Baptism and the Lord's Supper

Unit 8—The Commandments: The Second Table of the Law

Unit 9—Witnessing: Faith for Life

Who is God?

Does that seem like an easy question?
It isn't! Two out of three people do not know the answer.

How Do We Learn about God?

1 The world He created tells us something about God's existence.
(Natural Knowledge—see Psalm 19:1)

2 Your conscience tells you something about God's will.
(Natural Knowledge—see Romans 2:15)

3 Holy Scripture tells what is most important to know about God.
(Revealed Knowledge—see John 20:31)

What Is Different about Christianity?

It is about what _____ has done for _____

rather than what _____ have done for _____

The **TRIUNE** God is: _____,

_____,

_____.

Review

Trinity:	Grace:	Mercy:

Jesus Is Baptized

(Matthew 3:13–17; John 1:29–34)

God of Grace

giver

giver   giver

One God

Faith for Life

○ Today, in this place, ask yourself, "Why am I here?"

_____

_____

○ In your lifetime, on this earth, ask yourself, "Why am I here?"

_____

_____

○ Someday, in heaven, ask yourself, "Why am I here?"

_____

_____

Remember

"Jesus said to them, 'But who do you say that I am?' Simon Peter replied, 'You are the _____, the Son of the _____ God.'" (Matthew 16:15–16)

9

What are God's attributes?

Twelve Descriptors

Match these words that describe God's character with their definitions, printing the correct number on the blanks.

A. Spirit	___	1.	sinless and hating sin
B. Eternal	___	2.	all-knowing
C. Immutable	___	3.	a personal being without a body
D. Omnipotent	___	4.	full of pity, forgiving
E. Omniscient	___	5.	present everywhere
F. Omnipresent	___	6.	unchangeable
G. Holy	___	7.	without beginning and without end
H. Just	___	8.	righteous, desiring our welfare
I. Faithful	___	9.	keeping His promises
J. Good	___	10.	almighty, all-powerful
K. Merciful	___	11.	fair and impartial
L. Gracious	___	12.	showing undeserved kindness and compassion

Group Work

Read Psalm 103. In your own words, tell what God is like.

Review

BLESS	SIN
1. _____	1. _____
2. _____	2. _____
3. _____	3. _____

Show Us the Father

On the lines, write words and phrases that tell what Jesus is like.

John 14:8–11

Your Descriptors

List several of your positive qualities in the top half of the circle.

POSITIVE

NEGATIVE

Read Isaiah 64:6. What does this tell you about your positive qualities?

List several of your negative qualities in the bottom half of the circle.

Read 2 Corinthians 5:21. What does this say about your negative qualities?

Remember

"Come and see what God has done: He is _____ in His deeds toward the _____ _____ _____." (Psalm 66:5)

What is God's Word?
God Speaks to Us

God's Word Is
INSPIRED
2 Peter 1:21

God's Word Is
INERRANT
Psalm 18:30

God's Word Is
INVALUABLE
Romans 1:16–17

God's Word Is
INEXPRESSIBLE
1 Peter 1:8

Means of Grace

GOD

Holy
Baptism

Lord's
Supper

Sacraments

Review

Means of Grace _____

Sacraments _____

Prepare for Battle

EPHESIANS 6:10–17.   DEAR GOD, GUIDE AND PROTECT ME . . .

(v. 14a—belt of truth) _____

_____

(v. 14b—breastplate of righteousness) _____

_____

(v. 15—shoes of readiness by the gospel of peace) _____

_____

(v. 16—shield of faith) _____

_____

(v. 17a—helmet of salvation) _____

_____

(v. 17b—sword, the Word of God) _____

_____

Stay Connected

The armor of God is an analogy—it makes comparisons to prove a point. Here are several analogies about the importance of staying connected to God and His Word.

Consider someone in a hospital who has an IV that brings that person medication and nutrients. Staying connected is important because the IV is a lifeline. In an even greater way, it is important to stay connected to God and His Word because it is an eternal lifeline.

Here is another analogy. An electric cord needs to be connected to its power source. Likewise, we need to be connected to our power source, the Gospel, "for it is the power of God for salvation to everyone who believes" (Romans 1:16).

Even Jesus used analogies. Read His analogy about staying connected in John 15:5–11.

Grow in _____, _____, and _____. (See 2 Peter 3:18 and 2 Thessalonians 1:3.)

Remember

"Let the word of Christ _____ in you

_____." (Colossians 3:16)

13

How did God give His Word to us?

Primary Sources (Apostles & Prophets)

The main purpose of God's Word is "so that you may believe that Jesus is the Christ, the Son of God, and that by believing you may have life in His name" (John 20:31). Learn more about Scripture writers, their sources, audience, and specific purposes as your teacher guides you in filling in the missing words.

GOSPEL	SOURCE	AUDIENCE	PURPOSE
Matthew			Shows Jesus fulfilled Old Testament prophecies
Mark			Briefly describes Jesus' actions
Luke			Tells of Jesus' stories, miracles, and compassion
John			Explains Jesus' teachings rather than actions

Ultimate Source

Read these verses and highlight in your Bible the words that tell where the prophet got his information: Jeremiah 1:9; Jeremiah 7:1; Jeremiah 10:1; Jeremiah 11:1; Jeremiah 13:1; Jeremiah 14:8; Jeremiah 15:1; Jeremiah 16:1; and Jeremiah 17:19. (Look for more verses in Jeremiah, if time allows.) What did you learn from this Bible study?

_____

The Word Made Flesh

God loves us so much that He didn't just tell us His Word of salvation—He put that message into flesh, into human form, in Jesus, so that we could be certain of knowing Him and our salvation in Him. Read John 1:1–3 and 14. Each time you see "the Word," highlight it in your Bibles and print the name Jesus over it, because Jesus is *the Word made into flesh*.

Review

Primary Source: Spoken or written information from a person who actually witnessed or participated in an event.

Hope: The hope we have in Christ is the certainty (not just a wish) that our faith is based on. "Faith is the assurance of things hoped for, the conviction of things not seen" (Hebrews 11:1).

Incarnate: In the flesh, in human form.

What about You and Me Today?

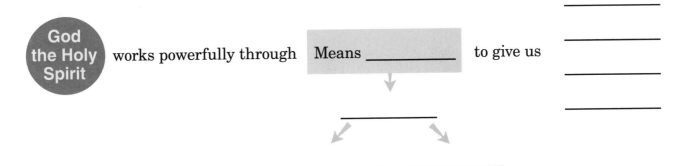

God the Holy Spirit works powerfully through **Means _____** to give us

_____

_____

_____

_____

_____   _____

Read John 16:13 and Romans 15:13. Consider that through the power of the Holy Spirit working in you through the Means of Grace, you, too, can hear God's voice (in the Scriptures), feel His healing in your life, be protected by His power, observe His loving kindness and blessings, and be saved by the body and blood of Jesus (just as happened to people over two thousand years ago)!

Caution!

Beware! The devil is continually working to harm us. 1 Peter 5:8 says, "Your adversary the devil prowls around like a roaring lion, seeking someone to devour." Read aloud these warnings about the dangers.

Galatians 1:6–7

2 Peter 2:1–3

2 Corinthians 11:13–15

How can we recognize if someone is telling us the truth or not? Go back to Scripture to find the answers.

Matthew 7:15–17 _____

_____

1 John 4:1–3 _____

_____

Remember

"There is salvation in no one else, for there is no other name under heaven given among men by which we must be saved" (Acts 4:12).

How has God preserved His Word through the years?

Cause  → Effect

2 Kings

Cause		Effect
21:19–22		The land of Judah had many altars to idols.
22:1–2		Josiah had a long, successful reign as king.
King Josiah commanded that the temple be repaired.		22:8
The Law of the Lord was read to the king.		22:11, 13
22:19–20		God gave a time of peace to the land of Judah.
The king read God's Word to the people.		23:3
Josiah removed all idols and restored the Passover.		23:25

God Blesses throughout History

	Fullness of Time	Spread of the Gospel	Rampant Illiteracy/ Barbarian Invasions
	Anno Domini	**100**	**400 . . .**
BC | AD	Jesus—Born, Lived, Died, Arose	Paul and the Early Church	Literate Church Leaders/ St. Patrick . . .

Review

God's Word endures (lasts, continues) because God preserves (protects, safeguards) it.

"Choosing a Church" Checklist

- ☐ Big building
- ☐ Cool music
- ☐ Happy, friendly pastor
- ☐ My friends go there
- ☐ Close to where we live
- ☐ _____

What about You and Me Today?

Errors in the Church **1500** Martin Luther	Government Controls **1830** Saxon Immigration to America	Modern Culture **21st Century** You and Me

Remember

"The grass _____ , the flower fades, but the word of our God will stand _____ ." (Isaiah 40:8)

How do we find things in the Bible?

Be a Berean

One day, Marcella said, "I go to school, and the teacher tells me about God; and I go to Sunday School, and the teacher there tells me about God; and then I go to church, where the pastor tells me about God. I'm tired of always being told what to say and do and learn." Her sister Mikayla responded, "Well, if you don't want people to always be telling you things, you better do a little digging and searching on your own. You'd better 'be a Berean.'" *What did Mikayla mean by that? Read Acts 17:11 to find out.*

Bible Dictionary

shep-herd
1. One who guards and tends sheep.
2. Someone who cares for and guides a group of people.

Bible Handbook

Shepherding A successful shepherd must be constantly on the alert to protect defenseless sheep from enemies such as wolves and dangers such as rocky cliffs. Sheep are good followers as long as they follow a good leader; if they follow another sheep that is careless, wandering, or panicked, they will follow right into troubles and dangers. Sheep need a guide because they often don't know where they are going, so it is important for the shepherd to lead them to safe areas where there is food and water. A good shepherd will be so familiar with his flock that he will know them individually, often calling them by name.

Bible Concordance

Shepherd

Psalm 23:1 The LORD is my *shepherd*; I shall not want.

Isaiah 40:11 He will tend his flock like a *shepherd*; he will gather the lambs in his arms.

Matthew 9:36 When he saw the crowds, he had compassion for them, because they were harassed and helpless, like sheep without a *shepherd*.

John 10:11 I am the good *shepherd*. The good shepherd lays down his life for the sheep.

John 10:14 I am the good *shepherd*. I know my own and my own know me.

1 Peter 2:25 For you were straying like sheep, but have now returned to the *Shepherd* and Overseer of your souls.

Revelation 7:17 For the Lamb in the midst of the throne will be their *shepherd*, and he will guide them to springs of living water.

Review

Which of the tools listed above

a. helps you find Bible verses containing a keyword? _____

b. helps you understand the meaning of a word? _____

c. provides extra background information? _____

Scripture Interprets Scripture

The best tool for understanding the Bible is the Bible itself. The Gospel writer Matthew understood this. Time and again, as he wrote about Jesus, he quoted from the Old Testament to show the connection: the New Testament is a continuation of the Old as Jesus fulfilled the promises of the Old Testament. Draw lines to match corresponding statements.

OLD TESTAMENT PROPHECIES	NEW TESTAMENT FULFILLMENT
"Rejoice greatly, O daughter of Zion! . . . Behold, your king is coming to you; righteous and having salvation is He, humble and mounted on a donkey." (Zechariah 9:9)	Matthew 1:22–23
"But you, O Bethlehem Ephrathah, who are too little to be among the clans of Judah, from you shall come forth for me one who is to be ruler in Israel." (Micah 5:2)	Matthew 2:5–6
"Behold, the virgin shall conceive and bear a son, and shall call His name Immanuel." (Isaiah 7:14)	Matthew 11:10–11
"Behold, I send My messenger, and he will prepare the way before Me." (Malachi 3:1)	Matthew 13:34–35
"'Awake, O sword, against My shepherd, against the man who stands next to Me,' declares the LORD of hosts. 'Strike the shepherd, and the sheep will be scattered.'" (Zechariah 13:7)	Matthew 21:4–8
"I will open my mouth in a parable; I will utter . . . things that we have heard and known." (Psalm 78:2–3)	Matthew 21:12–13
"My house shall be called a house of prayer for all peoples." (Isaiah 56:7)	Matthew 26:30–31

See Yourself in Scripture

In truth, we can see ourselves in the stories of sinners in the Bible, such as in the grumbling and complaining of the Israelites in the wilderness or the people who did not stop to help the man injured by thieves near Jericho. Pray that God would lead us to be like the tax collector in the temple who admitted his sinfulness, looked to God for mercy, and then returned home happy, knowing he was forgiven (see Luke 18:10–14). The words Paul wrote to young Timothy are important for us today as God's forgiven people who are enabled by the Holy Spirit to live for Him. See yourself in these verses, as Timothy is challenged to live in faith, in Jesus, guided by the Word (through the Holy Spirit). Read aloud 1 Timothy 4:12 and 2 Timothy 3:14–15.

Remember

"Your word is a lamp to my feet and a light to my path."

(Psalm 119:105)

How do we learn about Bible places and people?

More Tools

We can learn geographical background of many Bible stories by exploring a Bible atlas such as the one in the Appendix of this book. (What does *atlas* mean? See below.) What conclusions can you make from these maps of Bible lands?

_____

_____

_____

Mountains That Matter

MT. MORIAH	MT. SINAI	MT. CARMEL	MT. CALVARY	MT. OLIVET
Genesis 22:1–14	Exodus 19:16–20; 20:1–3	1 Kings 18:20, 30–39	(Golgotha) John 19:17–18	Acts 1:8–12

_____ _____ _____ _____ _____

_____ _____ _____ _____ _____

_____ _____ _____ _____ _____

_____ _____ _____ _____ _____

Review

Atlas: A collection of maps

Genealogy: The record of ancestry and descendents of a family

Timelines and Trees

We can learn about people by seeing where they fit in a timeline or a family tree. Here is the beginning of a family tree. Fill in your name, and the names of your parents and grandparents. Pray that God will bless your family. Then look at Jesus' genealogy (family tree) in Matthew 1.

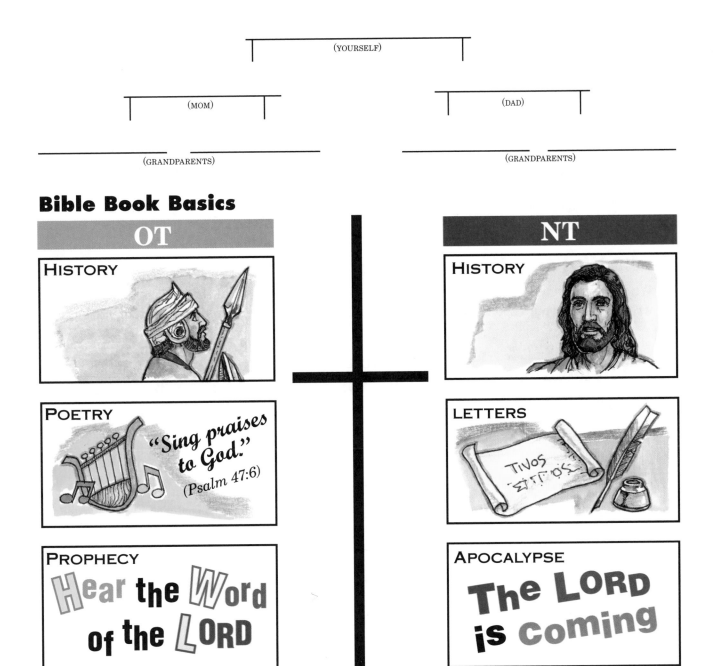

(YOURSELF)

(MOM)

(DAD)

(GRANDPARENTS)

(GRANDPARENTS)

Bible Book Basics

OT

HISTORY

POETRY

"Sing praises to God." (Psalm 47:6)

PROPHECY

Hear the Word of the LORD

NT

HISTORY

LETTERS

APOCALYPSE

The LORD is Coming

Remember

Jesus said, "You will be My witnesses in *Jerusalem* and in all *Judea* and *Samaria*, and to the end of the *earth*." (Acts 1:8, emphasis added)

How do we learn, apply, and use God's Word?

Why Study God's Word?

PAST → Jesus died on the cross to take away our sins.

PRESENT → What about Now?

FUTURE → Believers in Jesus will have eternal life in heaven.

God's Word: A Weapon/A Tool

What advice would you give someone (or yourself) when tempted in these ways to do wrong? Before you respond, look on the next page to learn how Jesus handled temptation.

I'm looking for the easy way.

I'm looking out for number one.

I'm looking to get whatever I want.

_____

_____

_____

_____

_____

_____

_____

_____

_____

_____

_____

_____

_____

_____

_____

Review

What do people want? Give examples.

Physical, material things _____

Fame, to be well-known _____

Fortune, money, wealth _____

Tempted, but Didn't Fall (Matthew 4:1-11)

TEMPTED BY	RESPONSE	A VERSE FOR YOU

Physical Wants

Matthew 4:4
Based on
Deuteronomy 8:3

_____
_____
_____
_____
Matthew 6:33

Fame

Matthew 4:7
Based on
Deuteronomy 6:16–17

_____
_____
_____
_____
Acts 5:29b

Fortune

Matthew 4:10
Based on
Deuteronomy 13:4

_____
_____
_____
_____
Luke 9:25

Remember

"Whatever is _____, whatever is _____, whatever is _____, whatever is _____, whatever is _____, whatever is _____, if there is any _____, if there is anything _____, think about these things." (Philippians 4:8)

⭐ BOTTOM LINE: IT'S NOT THE METHOD; IT'S THE MAN.

23

What are the Six Chief Parts of Christian Doctrine?

Where Do They Come From?

God's Word

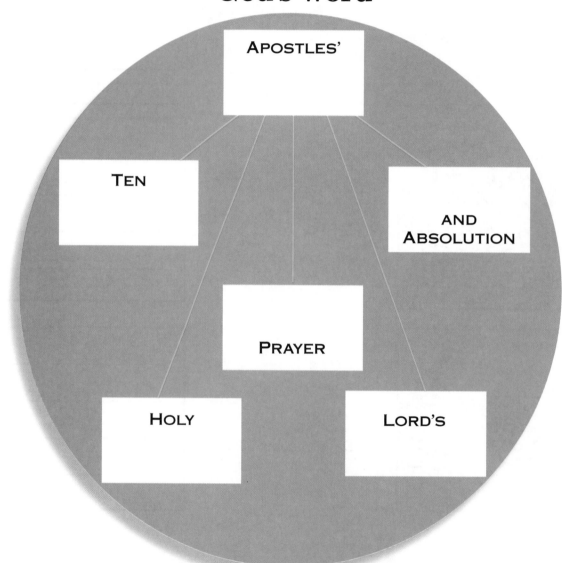

APOSTLES'

TEN

AND ABSOLUTION

PRAYER

HOLY

LORD'S

Review

Catechism: A book of instruction that summarizes basic principles in a question-and-answer format. Martin Luther's Small Catechism is based on the Six Chief Parts of Christian Doctrine, which are based on God's Word.

Enchiridion: This is the first, small section (approximately 10 percent) in *Luther's Small Catechism with Explanation*. It was written by Martin Luther and is often memorized by people who study God's Word. The enchiridion is then followed by an extended and deeper exploration and explanation of itself.

Worship: Based on the Six Chief Parts/Based on Scripture

Directions: List the page number where each of these is found in the liturgy of the Divine Service. Setting One in the *Lutheran Service Book*, and discuss each question.

1. God's Law and Commandments. Page _____.

   What sins are mentioned in the confessional prayer?

   _____

2. Confession/Absolution. Page _____.

   Why does Absolution immediately follow Confession?

   _____

3. Apostles' Creed. Page _____.

   What Creed can be used as an extended variation of the Apostles' Creed? (Compare similarities.)

   _____

4. The Lord's Prayer. Page _____.

   Are longer prayers better than shorter prayers?

   _____

5. Holy Baptism. Pages _____.

   Why is Baptism liturgy in a section separate from the regular Sunday liturgy?

   _____

6. The Lord's Supper. Page _____.

   Why is the Sacrament of the Altar listed as a part of the regular weekly liturgy?

   _____

Remember

"For I delivered to you as of *first importance* what I also received: that Christ died for our sins in accordance with the Scriptures, that He was buried, that He was raised on the third day in accordance with the Scriptures." (1 Corinthians 15:3, emphasis added)

What is God's Law?

Purposes of the Law

Stop Sign

Mirror

Guide

Look in Faith

Everyone who looks on the **P** **S** **O** **N** and believes should have in Him eternal life.

John 6:40

Review

Draw lines to match terms and definitions.

Condemnation	Admitting sorrowfully what you've done wrong
Consequence	Being judged and found guilty for your actions
Confession	The results of an action

Disobedience/Consequence/Deliverance
(Numbers 21:4–9)

_____ _____ _____

_____ _____ _____

Summary of the Ten Commandments

I. Respect God.

II. Respect God's name.

III. Respect God's Word.

IV. Respect leaders.

V. Respect life.

VI. Respect male/female.

VII. Respect property.

VIII. Respect reputations.

IX. Respect what you have.

X. Respect relationships.

Remember

"The wages* of sin is death,* but the free gift* of God is eternal life* in Christ Jesus our Lord." (Romans 6:23)

(what you deserve) (eternal separation from God) (grace) (life forever in heaven)

What is the Gospel?

GOSPEL GOOD NEWS

We are freed from the guilt, the punishment, and the power of sin and are saved eternally because of Christ's keeping the Law and through His suffering, death, and resurrection for us.

The Difference between Law and Gospel

	LAW	GOSPEL
Teaches:	• what to do • what not to do	• what God has done for our salvation • what God still does to bring us salvation
Shows:	• us our sin • the wrath of God	• our Savior, Jesus • the grace of God
Proclaims:	• to all people, but especially to the impenitent	• the grace of God to sinners who are troubled because of their sins

Review

Check which of these is a definition of the word *Gospel*.

1. The Bible books of Matthew, Mark, Luke, and John. _____

2. The story of Jesus' birth, life, death, and resurrection. _____

3. The promise of God in both the Old and New Testaments to forgive our sins and

offer eternal salvation through the Messiah (Jesus Christ). _____

Testify!

Councilman 1: Hey, why did we get called in here today? This is our day off!

Councilman 2: This better be good or I'm going right back home to take a nap.

Councilman 3: There was a major arrest of two men named Peter and John.

Councilman 4: What did they do wrong?

Councilman 5: They helped a crippled man to walk.

Councilman 6: What! Why arrest someone for something good like that? Maybe they can help my Aunt Edna!

Councilman 7: I'll tell you what they did wrong—they did it in the name and through the power of Jesus.

All Councilmen: What? I thought we got rid of that guy! Why won't He stay dead?

Councilman 8: Quiet down, the guards are bringing the two men in.

Councilman 9: "By what power or by what name did you do this?"

Peter: "If we are being examined today concerning a good deed done to a crippled man . . . let it be known to all of you and to all the people of Israel that by the name of Jesus Christ of Nazareth, whom you crucified, whom God raised from the dead—by Him this man is standing before you well."

Councilman 10: Good grief! These are uneducated, common men. How did they learn to speak like this?

Councilman 11: "What shall we do with these men?"

Peter: We speak in the name of Jesus for, "There is salvation in no one else, for there is no other name under heaven given among men by which we must be saved."

Councilman 12: Here is our judgment and order: you are "not to speak or teach at all in the name of Jesus."

John: "Whether it is right in the sight of God to listen to you rather than to God, you must judge, for we cannot help but speak of what we have seen and heard."

Councilman 13: Don't you ever give up? Well, this is not the end of the matter. We'll see you back in court again one of these days.

What happened next? Read aloud Acts 4:23–24, 29–31.
What happened next? Read aloud Acts 5:34–35, 38–40.
What happened next? Read aloud Acts 6:7.

PRAISE GOD !!

Remember

"I am not ashamed of the gospel, for it is the power of God for salvation to everyone who believes." (Romans 1:16)

What is the summary of the Law?

The First Commandment

You shall have no other gods. *What does this mean?*
We should fear, love, and trust in God above all things.

Him alone as highest being

Him with our lives

what displeases Him

to Him alone as our God

our lives to His service

our lives completely to His keeping

on Him for help in every need

Review

Use the words below to complete the phrases above. (Use the Appendix dictionary as needed.)

| Cling | Honor | Revere | Devote | Avoid | Rely | Commit |

Bible Story Review

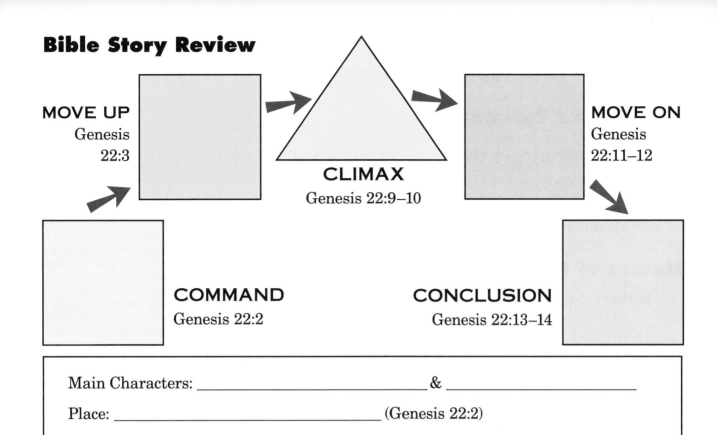

MOVE UP
Genesis 22:3

CLIMAX
Genesis 22:9–10

MOVE ON
Genesis 22:11–12

COMMAND
Genesis 22:2

CONCLUSION
Genesis 22:13–14

Main Characters: _____ & _____

Place: _____ (Genesis 22:2)

Remember

"They who wait for the LORD shall renew their strength; they shall mount up with wings like *eagles*; they shall run and not be weary; they shall walk and not faint." (Isaiah 40:31)

How do we honor God's name?

The Second Commandment

You shall not misuse the name of the Lord your God.

What does this mean? We should fear and love God so that we do not curse, swear, use satanic arts, lie or deceive by His name, but call upon it in every trouble, pray, praise, and give thanks.

Names of the One True God

On these stones, write the names of God found in these Bible verses.

Psalm 46:4   Psalm 47:7   Psalm 48:14

Psalm 62:2   Psalm 89:8   Isaiah 7:14

Isaiah 9:6   Jeremiah 23:6   Matthew 1:21

John 1:1   1 Timothy 6:15   Hebrews 4:14   Revelation 1:8

Review

1. Speaking evil of God or calling God's anger down on someone or something.

2. Calling on God to punish you if what you say is not true.

3. Calling on false spirits, the devil, horoscopes, fortune tellers, and so forth, ignoring and bypassing the truth of God's will.

4. Teaching false doctrine as if it came from God, or pretending to be a Christian.

No Contest (1 Kings 18:16–46)

BAAL

THE LORD GOD ALMIGHTY

CLAIMED TO BE:

rider of the clouds

god of thunderstorms

with goddess of the sea

provider of food crops

controller of nature

SCRIPTURAL TRUTH:

Psalm 104:1–3

Psalm 104:10–13, 16

Psalm 104:24–26

Psalm 104:27–30

Psalm 104:31–32

Saying God's Name

Good God	_____
O Lord	_____
Jesus Christ	_____
Great God in heaven	_____
For Christ's sake	_____

Remember

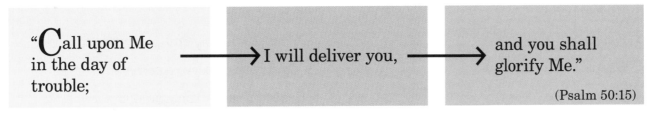

"Call upon Me in the day of trouble; → I will deliver you, → and you shall glorify Me."

(Psalm 50:15)

How do we remember the Sabbath?

The Third Commandment

Remember the Sabbath day by keeping it holy.

What does this mean?

We should fear and love God so that we do not despise preaching and His Word, but hold it sacred and gladly hear and learn it.

FATHER	SON	HOLY SPIRIT

What Is Worship?

W: _____ (orWd nad acSarmenst)

O: _____ (fOrefngi: salneTt nad rTsseaure)

R: _____ (eeRpntncae nad weRenla)

S: _____ (ngSi yHmsn fo aiPser)

H: _____ (nooHr nad seRptec)

I: _____ (nI Fellwoihps thiw rstCihanis)

P: _____ (yarP goTteher)

Review

(Draw lines to match meanings with terms.)

Remember •

Sabbath •

Despise •

Sacred •

• Neglect, ignore

• Honored as holy and dedicated to God

• Celebrate, observe a ceremony

• Rest and relief from cares and troubles

Worshiping Jesus

Palm Sunday
(Matthew 21:1–11)

Any Sunday—Divine Service
Lutheran Service Book

Service of Preparation	How are our hearts prepared?
Service of the Word	When do we hear God's Word?
Service of the Sacrament	How is Holy Week celebrated?

Dedicated (set apart, devoted) to Honor God

Music, art, and architecture are means that many people have used to express glory to God. These three pictures represent a Renaissance painting from the sixteenth century, a marble sculpture by Michelangelo, and the architecture of a Gothic cathedral in Europe. Research architecture dedicated to God by learning more about the great cathedrals of Europe.

© Shutterstock,Inc.

Remember

Look up the word *worship* in the concordance of this book. Choose a verse that you want to memorize and print it (and its reference) on the lines below.

_____

(_____)

How do we live a life of worship?

Faith Walk

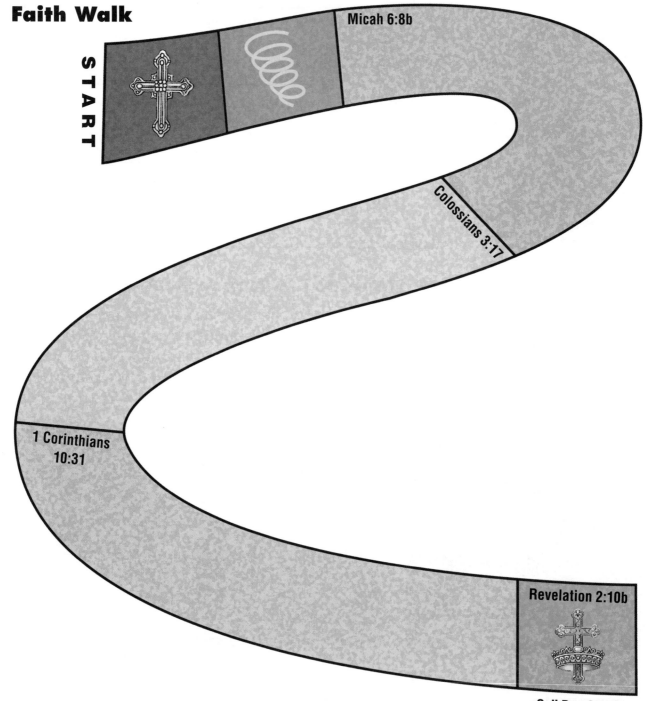

START

Micah 6:8b

Colossians 3:17

1 Corinthians 10:31

Revelation 2:10b

Soli Deo Gloria

Review

Walk: 1. Take steps 2. Behave or live in a certain way

Follow: 1. Walk behind 2. Try to imitate or emulate

Redeemer: Person who buys back

Ruth's Walk

START

MOAB
What was life like there?
Ruth 1:1–5

To → **BETHLEHEM**

Why did Ruth go?
Ruth 1:15–18

← **To** **FIELDS**

Why would life be difficult?
Ruth 1:19–21

How did God help them?
(Leviticus 19:9,10)
Ruth 2:2–3

How did Boaz help and why?
Ruth 2:8–12

What good news did Ruth bring home to Naomi?
Ruth 2:17–20

To ↓

A New Path in Life

Obed
Ruth 4:22

How did God bless Ruth and Naomi?
Ruth 4:13–15

Jesse
Matthew 1:5

David
Matthew 1:6

Time Passes →

The Savior →

Matthew 1:21–23

Remember

"_____ is everyone who _____ the LORD, who walks in His ways!" (Psalm 128:1)

37

Who is the Holy Spirit?

Filled with the Spirit

1. Look in the concordance in the back of this book for verses about the *Spirit*. Check off those that refer to people who received power from the Holy Spirit. What phrases do you see repeated? _____ with the Spirit; The Spirit _____ them.

2. How does the Holy Spirit come to you and me today? Through the Means_____. What are these? _____

   _____ .

   If this is how the Holy Spirit comes to us, empowers us, enables us, comforts us, refreshes us, and strengthens us, what does this tell us about our daily lives? _____

   _____

   _____

3. Whose work is more important? Discuss your answer.

   ❏ **Jesus**

   ❏ **Holy Spirit**

   ❏ _____

Review

Justification: We are rescued by Jesus' death and resurrection.

   From what? _____

   _____ ,

Sanctification: We are set free by the empowering gifts of the Spirit.

   What gifts? _____ .

"How Can These Things Be?" (John 3:9)

Nicodemus Questions Jesus (John 3:1–21)

List the verses from John 3 in which Jesus taught Nicodemus about these four things.

In which verse in John 3 can you find the answer to Nicodemus's question, "How can these things be?" _____

Living a Christian Life

1. **"I can do it!"** What is wrong with that statement? _____

_____

2. **"I'll never be able to do it."** What's wrong with that statement? _____

_____

_____

_____

3. HS → ME =   What do you think this means? _____

_____

Remember

"No one can say 'Jesus is _____' except in the _____

_____." (1 Corinthians 12:3)

How does the Holy Spirit bring us to faith?

Perfect Aim and on Target

Discuss how the Bible verses relate to the diagram you helped create with teacher directions.

1. Romans 5:5: "God's love has been poured into our hearts through the Holy Spirit who has been given to us." _____

2. Ephesians 6:17: "Take the . . . sword of the Spirit, which is the word of God."

   _____

3. Hebrews 4:12: "The Word of God is living and active, sharper than any two-edged sword." _____

Review

Sanctuary:
1. a consecrated place of peace and meditation; 2. a place set aside where God resides.

Do-Be-Do-Be-Do

Action verbs

_____
_____
_____
_____
_____
_____

MARY AND MARTHA
(Luke 10:38–42)

Being words

_____
_____
_____
_____
_____
_____

Lifetime Guarantee

I KNOW IT'S A LIFETIME GUARANTEE, BUT THE LIFETIME OF THIS CAR IS ONLY THREE MONTHS!

God's Word has more than a lifetime guarantee: the Word of the Lord endures forever! Look for the word *endures* in the concordance (in the Appendix) and find out what else lasts forever. _____
_____
_____
_____

How can we be certain of this? See 2 Corinthians 1:22. _____
_____

"The word of the Lord remains forever." (1 Peter 1:25)

Remember

Add the correct verbs to this Bible verse.

"_____ you not _____ that your body _____ a temple of the Holy Spirit within you, whom you _____ from God? You _____ not your own, for you _____ _____ with a price. So _____ God in your body." (1 Corinthians 6:19–20)

How does the Holy Spirit keep us in the faith?

Growing through the Means of Grace

SACRAMENTS

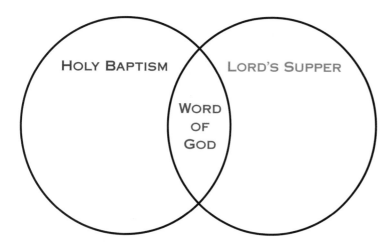

> The Holy Spirit works through the Means of Grace to offer faith, forgiveness, life, and salvation through our Savior, Jesus Christ.

1. God's Word connects to the visible element of water.
2. By the power of His Word, Christ gives His body and blood in, with, and under the bread and wine.
3. An event a person celebrates often.
4. A one-time event that is remembered daily.
5. Usually reserved for older children and adults after instruction.
6. For any age, including infants.
7. Observed by Jesus at the beginning of His ministry.
8. Instituted by Jesus at the end of His ministry.

Hearing the Word of God (Matthew 13:1–23)

The dry path represents people who hear God's Word but either ignore it or reject it, so God's Word never has a chance to take root and grow in their hearts and lives.	The rocky soil represents people who at first are glad to hear God's Word, but they are not firmly connected (rooted), so when troubles occur, their faith dries up and withers away.
The soil with weeds represents people who hear God's Word but have other things growing in their hearts too (such as the love of money and good times) until those things take over and choke out the Word.	Good soil represents the best growing conditions, in which the Holy Spirit is working through the Means of Grace; the faith and life of these people grow as they share good works for the glory of God.

Review

1. Fruit: The sweet part of a seed-bearing plant.   2. Fruit: The edible part of a plant.

3. Fruit: Results that have been produced.

What's Growing in Your Heart and Life?

Galatians 5:22–23

Remember

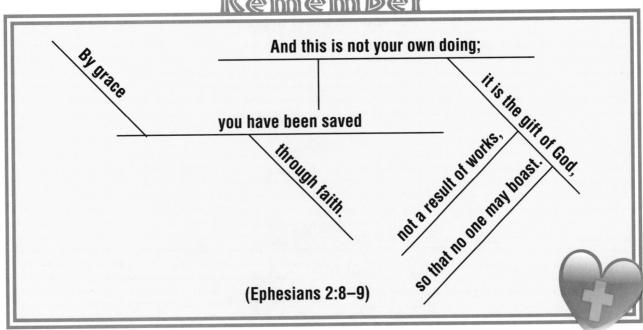

By grace

And this is not your own doing;

it is the gift of God,

you have been saved

through faith.

not a result of works,

so that no one may boast.

(Ephesians 2:8–9)

What does the sanctified life look like?

Check the Explanation

I believe that I cannot by my own reason or strength believe in Jesus Christ, my Lord, or come to Him; but the Holy Spirit has called me by the Gospel, enlightened me with His gifts, sanctified and kept me in the true faith.

From Martin Luther's explanation of the Third Article of the Apostles' Creed

Because we are weak and sinful, we cannot find, decide, choose, invite, create, or seek out God. So He comes to us! God the Holy Spirit finds us, chooses us, invites us, and seeks us out! In the box above, highlight words that describe four of the main tasks of the Holy Spirit. Then look up these related Bible verses and answer your teacher's questions about each one.

| a. Romans 1:16 | b. John 14:15; 15:26; 16:13 | c. 1 Corinthians 12:6, 11 | d. Philippians 1:6 |

The Call of Samuel

Let's consider an example: Samuel was possibly about your age; his teacher was Eli; Samuel was quick to help others; most important, God called him, setting him apart for a special purpose. Read this story in 1 Samuel 3:1–21, then give your responses to these comments.

1. "When God called Samuel, God spoke to him. God doesn't speak to His people today!" quipped Monique. _____

_____

2. "Okay," remarked Jaden. "God set Samuel apart for service. Has He set me apart? If so, for what purpose?" _____

_____

3. "In what ways did God train and equip Samuel to become a leader?" wondered Makayla. "How does He train and equip me?" _____

_____

_____

4. "I'm just a kid," said Kevin. "I think I'll have to wait until I'm a grown-up to serve the Lord in a special way." _____

_____

Review

1. **Enable:** When an outside source helps you to be_____
2. **Empower:** When an outside source gives you _____

Making a Spiritual Comparison

An *analogy* looks at something familiar and compares it to something else to help us understand a concept. With your teacher's help, look at this analogy and see how it compares with and helps us understand the way the Holy Spirit works in us.

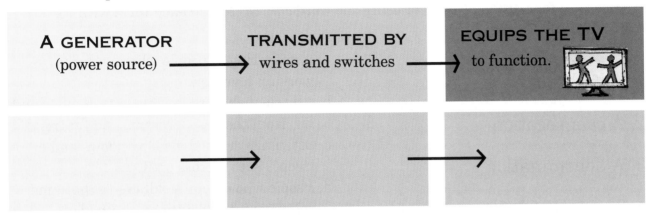

Equipped, Enabled, Empowered

Now we know that we cannot on our own live sanctified lives, but God makes it possible. Jesus takes away our sins (justifies us) and the Holy Spirit fills and equips us (sanctifies us) to live *righteously*.

So, back to the original question: What does the sanctified life look like?

"Be kind to one another, tenderhearted, forgiving one another, as God in Christ forgave you. Therefore be imitators of God as beloved children. And walk in love, as Christ loved us and gave Himself up for us." (Ephesians 4:32–5:2)

"Put on then, as God's chosen ones, holy and beloved, compassion, kindness, humility, meekness, and patience, bearing with one another and, if one has a complaint against another, forgiving each other; as the Lord has forgiven you, so you also must forgive. And above all these put on love." (Colossians 3:12–14)

"Encourage the fainthearted, help the weak, be patient with them all. See that no one repays anyone evil for evil, but always seek to do good to one another and to everyone. Rejoice always, pray without ceasing, give thanks in all circumstances; for this is the will of God in Christ Jesus for you." (1 Thessalonians 5:14–19)

"Set your minds on things that are above, not on things that are on earth. . . . And whatever you do, in word or deed, do everything in the name of the Lord Jesus, giving thanks to God the Father through Him. . . . Whatever you do, work heartily, as for the Lord and not for men." (Colossians 3:2, 17, 23)

Remember

"You were washed, you were _____ , you were _____ in the name of the Lord Jesus Christ and by the Spirit of our God."
(1 Corinthians 6:11)

What is the Church?

A Matter of Definitions

Here are four different ways of using the word *church*. Match each term with its definition.

1. A building

2. A congregation

3. A denomination

4. The Holy Christian Church

a. A gathering of people who regularly worship together.

b. All true believers in Christ, from near and far, from the past, present, and future.

c. Often has stained-glass windows and a steeple with a cross on it.

d. People who officially adhere to the same religious interpretations and belief systems, even though they might be far apart geographically.

A New Way of Looking at Things

Read Acts 10. Like all who studied and believed the sacred writings of the Old Testament in Leviticus, Peter carefully followed the dietary guidelines for what God's people should and shouldn't eat. However, as Peter was to learn, these laws were not to apply to New Testament believers (Colossians 2:16–17). This would serve as an object lesson for the removal of restrictions of another kind. While Old Testament believers limited their interactions with those who were not Jewish, God's message to Peter revealed that the gift of forgiveness, new life, and eternal salvation through Christ Jesus is for all people, Jew and Gentile alike.

Review

Ekklesia is the word for *church* used in the New Testament. It means "calling out" and describes those called out from the darkness of sin into the light of the Gospel: persons of various times, places, and backgrounds who have been called to faith in Jesus. Peter boldly preached the Good News to Jews from all over the world who had assembled for the feast of Pentecost in Jerusalem. Later, Peter would come face-to-face with a greater reality. God grace is not limited to Jewish people; God also wants Gentiles (those who are not Jews) to become members of His Church: the family of believers.

Review the events of Acts 10 as you identify each of the following statements as true or false.

____ 1. Cornelius, the Italian centurion, was well-known among the Jewish people for his wicked and impious acts (vv. 2, 22).

____ 2. The angel in Cornelius's vision revealed to Cornelius the exact location of Peter (vv. 5–6).

____ 3. Peter was experiencing hunger when he entered a trance in which he saw animals, birds, and reptiles (vv. 10–12).

____ 4. God spoke the same words to Peter three times in a vision (vv. 15–16).

____ 5. When the three men who had been sent by Cornelius arrived, Peter refused to invite them into the house because they were Gentiles (vv. 21–23).

____ 6. When Cornelius first met Peter, he fell at his feet and began to worship him (v. 25).

____ 7. Peter preached to Cornelius and his family and friends, telling them that although God is partial to the Jews, He also extends the Gospel of Christ to those of other people groups (vv. 34–35).

____ 8. Peter told the Gentiles that Jesus died on the cross and rose again, but he describes a spirit of Christ rather than a flesh-and-blood person (vv. 40–41).

____ 9. The Holy Spirit came directly upon the Gentiles in a way that did not relate with or connect to the Word of God (v. 44).

____ 10. Peter commanded that the Gentile believers be baptized (v. 48).

The Church in Action

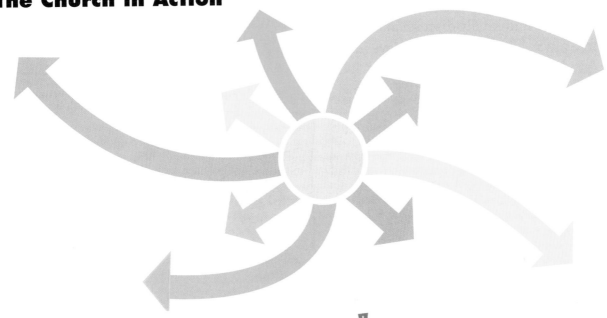

Remember

"For as in one body we have many members, . . . so we, though many, are one body in Christ." (Romans 12:4–5)

(Circle the words that are the title for this book.)

Why are there so many different types of Christian churches?

Divisions in the Church

1. What do you think causes disagreements in the Church? (See Romans 16:17–18.)

   _____

2. What attitude should we have toward fellow Christians as we try to resolve problems? (See 1 Peter 3:8; Ephesians 4:1–7.)

   _____

3. What is the ultimate standard for making decisions in the Church? (See John 17:17; 1 Corinthians 15:3; Hebrews 10:23; 1 Corinthians 16:13–14.)

   _____

   _____

Differences among Differences

Both of these situations show differences among people that lead to arguments. However, there is a big difference between these two kinds of differences. Which one is a matter of opinion that should be handled with reasonable discussion, compromise, and care for one another? Which is a matter faith and doctrine and should involve reasonable and kindly discussion that searches for truth and will not compromise on it, while always focusing on God's love and God's will?

Review

Protestant: _____

Reformation: _____

Denomination: _____

A History of Christianity

APOSTOLIC CHRISTIAN CHURCH (AD 30)				
EARLY CHRISTIAN CHURCH (AD 100)				
MEDIEVAL UNIVERSAL/CATHOLIC CHURCH (AD 476)				
GREEK ORTHODOX CHURCH (SPLIT AD 1054) ROMAN CATHOLIC CHURCH				
THE REFORMATION (AD 1517)				
LUTHERAN CHURCH	DUTCH REFORMED	MENNONITES	QUAKERS	METHODISTS
CALVINISTS	CHRISTIAN REFORMED	AMISH	PURITANS/PILGRIMS	CHURCH OF THE NAZARENE
CHURCH OF SCOTLAND	ANABAPTISTS	CHRISTIAN AND MISSIONARY ALLIANCE	CONGREGATIONALISTS	PENTECOSTALS
CHURCH OF IRELAND	BAPTISTS	CHURCH OF ENGLAND	VINEYARD MOVEMENT	EVANGELICAL FREE

A History of Christianity

God's Word teaches us that there is only one true Church, made up of those who believe in Jesus as the Savior of the world. Jesus alone is the foundation of the true Church.

However, Satan remains alive and active. He likes nothing better than to create conflict among Christ's followers. Dividing and conquering is a strategy he often uses successfully to hamper the Church in its mission to spread the Gospel.

Following the birth of the Christian Church at Pentecost, the apostles established Christian churches throughout the world. Paul started one such church in Corinth, an important cosmopolitan center in the ancient world. Eventually, with the growth of more and more churches, Christianity began to organize as a catholic (meaning universal) Church. In the eleventh century, the Christian Church split over differences in doctrine and authority. Two churches emerged: the Eastern Church, centered in Constantinople, and the Western Church, headquartered in Rome.

In the sixteenth century, Martin Luther sought to return the Church to the doctrine and practices of the Early Church, when God's Word was the source for all teachings. When the Church refused to reform and expelled Luther, he had no choice but to establish a new denomination. Many followed Luther, but some disagreed with Luther's reforms. Some sought to remove the art and liturgical elements associated with the Catholic Church. A group known as the Anabaptists believed God revealed Himself to them directly, outside of God's Word; they denied infant Baptism and believed the bread and wine merely symbolized Christ's body and blood. At the time of Luther, other reformers, such as Zwingli, Calvin, Knox, and Cranmer, left the Catholic Church to begin denominations of their own. These Protestant denominations became known as Reformed churches. Although church bodies may differ significantly, they all may still be classified as Christian churches if they believe in the teachings of the three Creeds, professing belief in the Trinity and in Jesus as the Son of God and Savior of the world.

Remember

"No one can lay a foundation other than that which is laid, which is Jesus Christ." (1 Corinthians 3:11)

What can we learn from heroes of the faith?

Directions: Label the ribbons with the names of people who are your heroes.

What difference does it make? See Philippians 4:8.

_____

Got any suggestions? See Ephesians 5:1–2.

_____

Elijah: A Biblical Hero

1. Elijah bravely accused an evil king of doing wrong.
2. Elijah confidently challenged 450 Baal prophets to a test.
3. Elijah outran a chariot pulled by horses.
4. Elijah crawled into a cave to hide.

Review

Imitate: To copy the actions or behaviors of someone else.

Emulate: To strive for accomplishments similar to someone else.

Reflect: To mirror the likeness or image of someone else.

Our Hero

I GIVE UP!

I'VE HAD ENOUGH!

FIRE   ANGEL   DIE   WIND   HOREB   EARTHQUAKE   BAAL   WHISPER

a. Elijah felt persecuted and disillusioned; he was discouraged and wanted to _____ (1 Kings 19:4).

b. Strengthened by the food and water the _____ provided, Elijah traveled forty days and forty nights to Mount _____, also known as Mount Sinai or the mountain of God (vv. 5–8).

c. Elijah stood at the mouth of the cave in which he was staying and witnessed a strong _____, an _____, and _____ but God was not in any of these (vv. 9–12).

d. God came to Elijah in a low _____ of a voice, which asked, "What are you doing here, Elijah?" (v. 13).

e. God told Elijah of the work he still needed to do and encouraged him with some revealing facts: Elijah was not alone; there were still seven thousand in Israel who had not worshiped _____ (vv. 14–18).

The Making of a Hero

Heroes give us a picture of the person we would like to become. They have the qualities we ourselves would like to have. Jesus is the ultimate hero. He provides an example of excellence. As the Son of God, Jesus was the one and only holy person who ever lived. He performed the ultimate sacrificial act by giving His life to save us from sin and eternal punishment. He demonstrated His limitless power by coming back to life after submitting to death. His limitless power remains at work today, enabling ordinary people (such as you and me!) to live as followers of the true God. Consider that the definition of a hero is **someone who has a sense of purpose and gives extra effort to achieve something, usually for the benefit of other people.**

When you pick up something an elderly person dropped, he sees you as his hero. When you take time to play with a little child, she sees you as her hero. When you are friendly to someone who has no friends, it may take courage, but you are a hero. List ways you could be a hero to someone else; identify whom you will help, how you will do something extra for his or her benefit, and plan when you can do this. Be very specific and make a commitment to follow through with this plan, always doing kindness for others as a response to what Jesus has already done for you!

_____

_____

_____

Remember

"Be strong and courageous. Do not be frightened, and do not be dismayed, for the LORD your God is with you wherever you go." (Joshua 1:9)

Who was Martin Luther?

Created, Redeemed, and Called by God

The fifteenth-century world into which Martin Luther was born differed greatly from the world of today. Everyone in his European hometown of Eisleben, in what is now Germany, held the same worldview. They were told what to believe by the priests of the Medieval Church. Few could read, and even if they could read, Bibles were scarce and written in Latin, a language known only by those with much education.

By and large, the people were fearful and superstitious. They believed that forces of evil could be kept away through pious actions, such as visiting holy places and repeating holy words without even giving thought to their meaning. The Medieval Church had fallen away from the teachings of God's Word, which explains salvation, forgiveness of sins, and the power for a new life as gifts of God. These gifts were earned by Jesus through His innocent life and death on the cross to pay for the sins of all people. Like others alive at this time, Martin's hardworking and strict parents taught their children to serve and obey God so that they might go to heaven when they died. People were afraid of God and His punishment for their sins; they thought they had to do good works to gain God's favor.

Once, when caught in a violent thunderstorm, young Martin prayed that

if he survived the storm he would become a monk and live a life of poverty and obedience in service to God. As a monk and a worker in the Church, Martin continued his education in theology. As he studied, he was able to read the Bible on his own. From God's Word, Martin learned God was a loving God who had created him and given him freely the gifts of forgiveness and salvation. In Habakkuk 2:4, he read, "The righteous shall live by his faith." God called Martin through His Word and made him God's own dear child in Baptism. In this same way, God has called each of us to be His own dear children.

Review

Martin Luther lived during these time periods. Match them with their definitions.

Medieval	An era of great changes in culture and academics, led by greater individual independence of thought.
Reformation	A period of many centuries of domination by royalty and clergy.
Renaissance	A point in history where God blessed the Church with reformers who bravely proclaimed a return to the pure truth of God's Word, especially in the Gospel of salvation through Christ Jesus.

The Seal of The Lutheran Church—Missouri Synod (LCMS)

This is the official seal of our church denomination. It is very much like a family tree, explaining who we are. This one picture holds a lot of meaning.

In the center at the bottom is Luther's coat of arms, flanked on the right by the year of the founding of the Synod: AD 1847. Immediately above Luther's coat of arms appears the word *Concordia*. This is the name of the collection of confessional writings gathered together in the book of that name, compiled in the year 1580.

The primary emphasis of the seal is the great blue shield, which runs through the center. The shield is symbolic of the faith of the Christian (Ephesians 6:16). On the shield, the cross is central and most emphatic, because the faith and preaching of the Church is centered in Christ crucified. On the shield there also appears in small lettering the earliest creed of the Christian Church, *Jesus Christus Dominus Est* (Jesus Christ is Lord), in order that the name *Jesus Christ* might appear in the very heart of this seal.

Below these letters appear three equilateral crosses, symbolic of the Holy Trinity. In the three corners of the shield are three stars as symbols of the three creeds: the Apostolic, the Nicene, and the Athanasian. The shield itself is set on a pattern of vines and grapes, which is a reminder of the Savior's words in John 15:5. Spaced on each side of the shield, left and right, are six stars, which stand for the six specifically Lutheran Confessions of the Church: (1) the Augsburg Confession, (2) the Apology (Defense) of the Augsburg Confession, (3) the Smalcald Articles, (4) the Small Catechism of Luther, (5) the Large Catechism of Luther, (6) the Formula of Concord.

Around the inner circle are found the constant Lutheran emphases: Sola Scriptura, Sola Gratia, Sola Fide (Scripture alone, grace alone, faith alone).

This is the legal and corporate seal of the official organization known as the The Lutheran Church—Missouri Synod. For that reason, it is to be used only by the International Headquarters of the church body and not by individual churches or schools that are parts of this body.

The seal was designed by Rev. A. R. Kretzmann of Chicago, and the drawing is by Walter Geweke, also of Chicago.

Remember

"**P**roclaim the excellencies of Him who called you out of darkness into His marvelous light." (1 Peter 2:9b)

What did Martin Luther do?

Martin Luther Takes a Stand

Though his father wanted him to become a lawyer, Martin Luther felt called to serve the Church. He did serve, first as a monk, then as a priest and theology professor at a university. Through his study of God's Word, Martin came to recognize that God loves people and that He gives forgiveness and salvation as a free gift to all who believe in Jesus. The gifts Jesus provides for free we could not earn even if we tried.

The Church in Luther's day taught something very different. Although the Church taught that Jesus died for the sins of the world, it also taught that people could buy forgiveness through indulgences, even before committing sins. Indulgences were official pieces of paper guaranteeing forgiveness, issued with the support and backing of the pope himself. Luther became concerned that many who purchased indulgences showed no sorrow over their sins. In addition, Luther could find nothing in God's Word promoting indulgences and other Church practices, such as praying to Mary and the saints.

Luther argued against those teachings and practices of the Church that had no basis in God's Word. His ideas spread quickly, because the recently-invented printing press made widespread distribution of his books possible. Eventually, Luther was called to a trial before the political leader of the day, Emperor Charles V. When he was asked to take back his statements against the Church, Luther replied, "Unless I am convinced by Scripture and plain reason, I do not accept the authority of popes and councils, for they have contradicted each other. My conscience is captive to the Word of God. I cannot and I will not recant anything, for to go against my conscience is neither right nor safe. Here I stand. God help me. Amen."

Luther boldly stood up for what he knew to be right against a crowd of powerful rulers who accused and threatened him. He trusted in God's truth and power to give him strength.

Review

Means of Grace: _____

Sacraments: _____

When Doing the Right Thing Is Difficult

Martin Luther was extraordinary in his Spirit-led boldness to stand up to powerful leaders when they were doing wrong, but he certainly wasn't the only one to do so. This situation arises time and again throughout history, because we live in a sin-filled world. Let's look back to a somewhat-similar situation in Old Testament times. In these Scripture passages, we will see that a powerful leader, King Saul, imposed his own will on the worship of the people. This is similar to the Church leaders of Martin Luther's day, who imposed on the people their false teachings about buying forgiveness through indulgences. In both situations, God raised up and emboldened a leader to accuse those in power of wrongdoing—Samuel in the Bible and Luther in the 1500s—and both put themselves in great danger by doing so.

Saul had been chosen by God to be the leader and king of God's people. At first, Saul trusted God, but then he gave in to self-will and disobeyed God's commands. Begin by reading the words of Samuel in 1 Samuel 12:24–25.

Continue with Saul's disobedience and Samuel's rebuke in 1 Samuel 13:1–14. Saul sacrificed an offering to God. What was wrong with that?

_____

_____

_____

Continue by reading 1 Samuel 15:1–23. Once again, Saul tried to cover up his sinfulness behind the pretense of wanting to offer a sacrifice to God. Saul disobeyed God's command, and he lied about it. He had intended to keep the best for himself. What is more important to God than offerings and sacrifices?

_____

_____

Remember

"Create in me a clean heart, O God, and renew a right spirit within me." (Psalm 51:10)

What is the Lutheran Church?

The Lutheran Church follows the teachings of Martin Luther, but Luther would be the first to say that his teachings were not his own. His teachings and thoughts were based on Scripture: the very words of God Himself. Luther's teachings were not new; he proclaimed that the Church should uphold the old teachings of the prophets and apostles and stay true to Scripture alone, not adding to it and not reinventing it. Let's go back to Old Testament times and look at another important leader who spoke to the people about following the truth of God's Word.

Back to Old Testament Times

God's Old Testament people followed dynamic, powerful leaders such as Moses, who guided them by God's Word. After the death of God's servant Moses, God appointed Joshua to lead His people into the Promised Land. Once they had crossed the Jordan River and entered Canaan, it was the task of the people to conquer those who lived there and to claim the region as their own. When Joshua was old, he gathered Israel's leaders together to speak to them. He reminded them of how God had given them victory over their enemies. He told the people to remain faithful to God and to obey Him.

Joshua said, "And now I am about to go the way of all the earth, and you know in your hearts and souls, all of you, that not one word has failed of all the good things that the LORD your God promised concerning you. All have come to pass for you; not one of them has failed. . . . Now therefore fear the LORD and serve Him in sincerity and in faithfulness. Put away the gods that your fathers served beyond the River and in Egypt, and serve the LORD. And if it is evil in your eyes to serve the LORD, choose this day whom you will serve, whether the gods your fathers served in the region beyond the River, or the gods of the Amorites in whose land you dwell. But as for me and my house, we will serve the LORD" (Joshua 23:14; 24:14–15).

1. Draw a rectangle around Joshua's words that indicated he expected soon to die.
2. Highlight in yellow the words of Joshua that remind us of how God keeps His promises.
3. Circle the sentence in which Joshua tells the people to fear and serve God.
4. Highlight in orange or pink the words in which Joshua promises that he and his family will serve the Lord.

Review

Lutherans: People who agree with the doctrines Luther taught about faith, grace, Scripture, and salvation only through Christ Jesus.

On to Sixteenth-Century Times

When false teachings (such as praying to saints or the need to earn your own salvation) were added to the Church teachings, Martin Luther tried to lead people back to the truth of God's Word in the Scriptures. However, the Church of Martin Luther's day refused to listen him. They would not agree to rely solely upon God's grace through faith in Christ as God's Word teaches. Luther and his followers had no choice but to begin a church body of their own. In our modern world, where there are so many different kinds of Christian churches, beginning a new church body does not seem all that remarkable. In contrast, early sixteenth-century Europe knew only one main Christian denomination, and its headquarters were in Rome.

Following their dynamic separation from the Medieval Catholic Church, Luther and his followers were referred to as Protestants. Luther and the others who left the Medieval Catholic Church were regarded as protesters. Luther was even declared an outlaw.

Breaking away from the church came with great conflict. Those who left the Catholic Church disagreed not only with the church but also with one another. When the Catholic Church realized how many people were abandoning it, they took steps to bring the people back. Wars and persecutions resulted. Many lost their lives.

Still, Luther did not set out to create a new church body. He simply wanted to restore the teachings and practices set forth in the Bible. People began to refer to Luther's followers as Lutherans. Luther was humble. He did not want people to focus on him but rather to follow Jesus. Nevertheless, the name stuck. Millions of Christians around the world today call themselves Lutherans. Discuss these questions.

1. Under what circumstances is protesting right (see Acts 5:29)?

2. When is it wrong to protest (Romans 13:1)?

3. What is a Protestant?

4. What about Luther's teachings makes them old?

5. What about Luther's teachings makes them new?

Remember

"But as for me and my house, we will serve the LORD."

(Joshua 24:15b)

Why is the Reformation important?

New Understandings about Old Truths

The Reformation at the time of Martin Luther had many important results, but the single most important thing was the recognition that we are saved only and solely by Jesus. He *justified* us through His death and resurrection. Any good works we try to do cannot save us. Only the work of Jesus saves.

1. What is wrong with this statement? "Jesus forgives my sins, but I must be a good person and go to church so I can be sure to go to heaven." (See Romans 3:23; Hebrews 11:6.) _____

   _____

   _____

2. What is wrong with this statement? "I believe in Jesus, so I don't bother about good works because they aren't important." (See James 2:17, 22.) _____

   _____

   _____

3. Comment on what is right about this statement. "First, we are justified completely by Jesus' work of salvation; sanctification follows as the Holy Spirit continues to work in us to lead us to good works." (See Ephesians 2:8–10; Philippians 1:6.) _____

   _____

   _____

He Just Didn't Get It!

Matthew 19:16–26 tells about a young man who thought he could earn God's favor and be saved by his good works. He asked Jesus, "Teacher, what good deed must I do to have eternal life?" (v. 17). After clarifying that only God understands goodness, Jesus told the young man to keep the commandments. Discuss what followed.

1. What did the rich young man say in response (v. 20)?

   _____

2. What did Jesus then tell the young man to do (v. 21)?

   _____

3. Describe the rich young man's reaction and what came first in his heart (v. 22).

   _____

   _____

4. What question about salvation did the disciples then ask (v. 25)?

   _____

5. What impossible means of salvation was Jesus referring to (v. 26)?

   _____

   _____

6. Jesus, as true God, did what seemingly impossible thing to save us?

   _____

   _____

   _____

Review

Justification: *What God does for us through Jesus.*

Sanctification: *What God does in us through the Holy Spirit.*

Five Pillars?

People often talk about the five pillars of the Reformation, meaning the five strong main ideas that called for and supported a change in the Church. However, that might not be the best way to consider these ideas, because one of the five is the foundation of all the rest and most important of all. That one would be *Solus Christus*. Discuss what important truths this illustration is telling us. Then write the English translation below each Latin phrase.

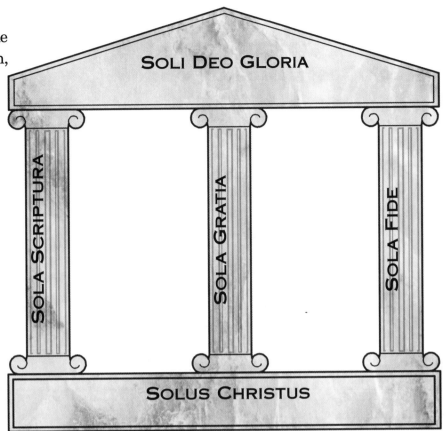

Pivotal Points

This timeline indicates some of the pivotal points in history. These points had a great impact on events that followed. Very often, the people and events created great changes or caused new directions for the future.

What was pivotal about the life and times of Moses? What pivotal changes occurred at the time of Martin Luther? The most significant pivotal point in time is not labeled on the timeline. Draw a large cross there. Why is the life, death, and resurrection of Jesus the most significant point in all of history? _____

_____

_____

Remember

"He saved us, not because of works done by us in righteousness, but according to His own mercy, . . . so that being justified by His grace we might become heirs according to the hope of eternal life." (Titus 3:5, 7)

Can I become a saint?

Job Description of a Saint

○ Designated so and canonized by the Church

○ Superhuman

○ Has miraculous power to help others

○ Hears prayers

○ Mediates between God and people

○ Should be worshiped

○ A good person

○ A believer who died and has gone to heaven

Listen to Luther

> Just as we should not deny that we are baptized and Christians, so we should not deny or doubt that we are holy. . . . For when Christians call themselves holy after Christ, this is not arrogance; it is honoring and praising God. For thereby we do not praise the malodorous holiness of our own works but His Baptism, Word, grace, and Spirit, which we do not have of ourselves; He gave them to us. . . .
>
> I have often said that the kingdom of Christ is nothing but pure forgiveness, a kingdom that deals only with sins and always wipes them away, covers them, and cleanses us of them. . . . To call yourself a saint is, therefore, no presumption but an act of gratitude and a confession of God's blessings. . . .
>
> Only beware of the ambition to make yourself holy by your own works. . . . [God] wants to sanctify you and will have no directions about sanctification from you. Be sure to give this some thought.
>
> —Martin Luther (*What Luther Says* § 3977–79)

Review

Saint: _____

_____

Lied and Denied (A Sinner)

(Based on John 18:15–17, 25–27)

SINNER

When Jesus was arrested and placed on trial at the high priest's house, Peter followed. A servant girl said to Peter, "You're His disciple!" Peter denied it, saying "I am not!" He moved away from the questioning stares and tried to warm himself near a fire of burning coals. Some of the officers and guards stood there also. One person said, "Aren't you one of Jesus' disciples?" Peter lied, "No, I am not!" Then a servant of the high priest himself said, "You sound like you're from the same area as Jesus; didn't I see you with Him earlier tonight in the garden?" This time Peter cursed as he denied Jesus once again. When a rooster crowed, Peter remembered Jesus' warning. He was ashamed of himself. He knew he'd broken his relationship with Jesus.

Three for Three (A Saint)

(Based on John 21:1–17)

SAINT

After Easter, Peter and his friends saw Jesus on the beach, fixing breakfast. Jesus asked Peter, "Do you truly love Me?" Peter did not deny Jesus this time. He said, "Yes, Lord, you know that I love you." Jesus replied, "Feed My lambs." Again Jesus asked Peter, "Do you love Me?" Again Peter answered, "Yes." Jesus replied, "Tend My sheep." A third time, Jesus asked Peter, "Do you love Me?" When Peter answered, "Yes," Jesus told Peter, "Feed My sheep." Just as Peter had denied Jesus three times, Jesus now reinstated Peter three times, forgiving Peter and commissioning him to tell others the Gospel.

Remember

"Now He has reconciled you by Christ's physical body through death to present you holy in His sight, without blemish and free from accusation." (Colossians 1:22 NIV)

GOD THE FATHER'S GRACIOUS GIFTS: THE FIRST ARTICLE

What does it mean to call God "Father"?

God, the Father Almighty

We say in the Apostles' Creed, "I believe in God, the Father Almighty, Maker of heaven and earth." What does that mean for your life? In the arrow with rough edges, list situations where people might find it troublesome, worrisome, or even alarming that God is our almighty Father. In the graceful, colorful arrow, list times when people might find that truth comforting, calming, and even a relief.

Knowing God
is my almighty Father
worries me when . . .

Knowing God
is my almighty Father
brings me peace when . . .

Review

ALMIGHTY

This adjective means having all power and unlimited might.
Body builders may be strong. Earthly rulers may be powerful. Only God is almighty.

What a Family!

Match each Bible reference to the scene it describes. Write the letters in the small answer boxes.

| Exodus: | a. 15:1–5 | b. 15:22–24 | c. 15:25–27 | d. 16:1–3 | e. 16:9–18 |
| | f. 16:19–29 | g. 16:31–36 | h. 17:1–4 | i. 17:5–7 | |

Children of Israel: Full of Complaints and Disobedience

God the Father: Full of Grace and Mercy

FOR FORTY YEARS

In the last box, draw a picture of the greatest example of God's grace and mercy for His people.

Remember

"See what kind of love the Father has given to us, that we should be called children of God." (1 John 3:1)

How did all things come to be?

Perplexing Puzzle?

Directions: Draw lines to match the following "if" statements with the correct "then" statements.

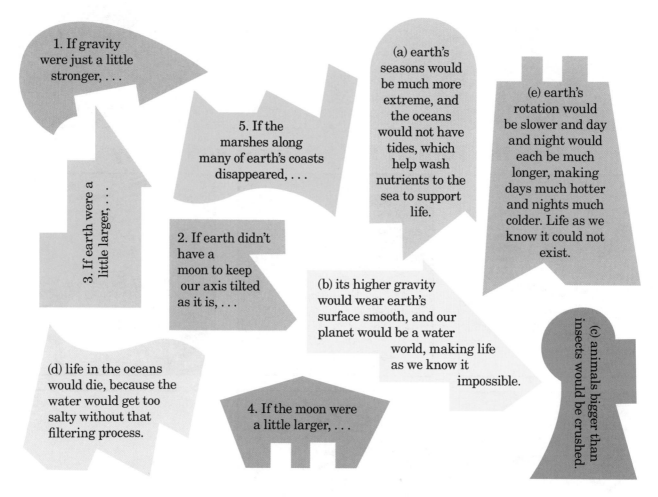

1. If gravity were just a little stronger, . . .

5. If the marshes along many of earth's coasts disappeared, . . .

(a) earth's seasons would be much more extreme, and the oceans would not have tides, which help wash nutrients to the sea to support life.

(e) earth's rotation would be slower and day and night would each be much longer, making days much hotter and nights much colder. Life as we know it could not exist.

3. If earth were a little larger, . . .

2. If earth didn't have a moon to keep our axis tilted as it is, . . .

(b) its higher gravity would wear earth's surface smooth, and our planet would be a water world, making life as we know it impossible.

(d) life in the oceans would die, because the water would get too salty without that filtering process.

4. If the moon were a little larger, . . .

(c) animals bigger than insects would be crushed.

The "puzzle" of making a beautiful, comfortable home for people on our planet involved getting thousands and thousands of details just right. The five facts above are just a few of these considerations. Every detail works together with other details to make life possible on earth. Some people want to conclude this is all a coincidence. How likely do you think that is? What causes order rather than random chaos?

Review

Ex Nihilo (eks-**nee**-hoe-low): Latin for "out of nothing."
God created the universe *ex nihilo*. (Note: God's Word not only says something, it accomplishes what it says!)

Creation:
Formed and Filled

D-1

D-2

D-3

D-4

D-5

D-6

A New Creation

Directions: Read Revelation 21:1–4; 22:1–5. Draw the tree that your mind imagines.

Remember

"According to [God's] promise we are waiting for new heavens and a new earth in which righteousness dwells." (2 Peter 3:13)

Why do we need new heavens and a new earth?

What do angels do?

Detecting Angels: Then

We cannot see, hear, touch, or otherwise prove that angels exist. The Bible doesn't try to prove it. Instead, it describes the holy angels and gives us clues about who they are and what they do. The word *angel* appears almost three hundred times in the Bible. Thirty-three of the Bible's sixty-six books mention angels and their work. This tells us how important they are. Use the following Bible verses to collect clues about angels. Then use these facts to form conclusions about who they are and what they do.

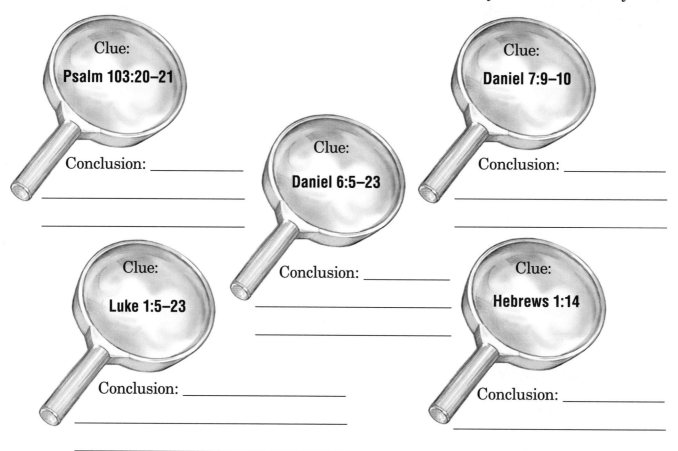

Clue:
Psalm 103:20–21
Conclusion: _____
_____
_____

Clue:
Daniel 6:5–23
Conclusion: _____
_____
_____

Clue:
Daniel 7:9–10
Conclusion: _____
_____
_____

Clue:
Luke 1:5–23
Conclusion: _____
_____
_____

Clue:
Hebrews 1:14
Conclusion: _____
_____
_____

Review

Angel: A spirit being created by God, having a mind and will but no physical body (though at times, for God's purposes, angels have taken on human form). There are both good and evil angels.

Cherubim (*chair-uh-bim*), *plural:* Angels of a specific rank or grouping; in Hebrew, the word implies nearness, perhaps indicating the cherubim's nearness to God. These angels are sometimes described as having four wings.

Seraphim (*sair-uh-fim*), *plural:* Angels of a specific rank or grouping; in Hebrew, it means "the burning ones," perhaps because the seraphim burn with love for God and zeal to serve Him. These are sometimes described as having six wings.

Detecting Angels: Now

Most of the time, angels are invisible. We can't detect them with a telescope or a microscope or a Geiger counter. But look around the classroom. God's angels are here! They have come at His command to protect and care for you. Choose one of these story starters or one of your own that tells of a real incident in which you feel God's angels were helping you. Think about it, and then write or tell your own story for your class. How might God's holy angels have been involved in it? (Note: If you don't have a story, that's all right, but start looking for one; they are all around you!)

- It was a very close call. I didn't see the danger at first, but . . .

- It was just a normal day. I was with my family and felt totally safe, but then . . .

- It wasn't just a matter of good luck. I know God and His angels helped me when . . .

_____

_____

_____

_____

When we are under the protection of God, there is no doubt that we are also under the safekeeping and guardianship of the angels, who are present with those who are encountering dangers in life and who conduct the dead to the place of peace and rest. . . . These things should . . . stir us up gladly to hear and love the Word, . . . [knowing] that we are covered by the protection of the angels.

—Martin Luther (LW 6:41–42)

Remember

"[God] will command His angels concerning you to _____

_____. On their hands they will

_____ , lest you strike your foot against a stone."

(Psalm 91:11–12)

Who is the devil?

The Bible states that Satan and his demons are real beings, as real as the holy angels, as real as you and me, as real as God Himself. The Bible says Satan is our sworn enemy. In Baptism, God claims us as His own. That makes it possible for us to renounce the devil and all his works and all his ways.

God gives us new life, but He never promises that new life will be easy here on earth. In fact, the Bible pictures it as a battle. In the battle between good and evil, light and darkness, we now fight on the side of Jesus, the King of kings, and His holy angels. Jesus has already won, but until He returns to take us to heaven, we're assaulted in ongoing skirmishes. The devil can't win the final victory, but he still tries to do as much damage as possible. For this reason, we need to know the devil's weapons and tactics. Even more important, we need to know the weapons and tactics God has given us!

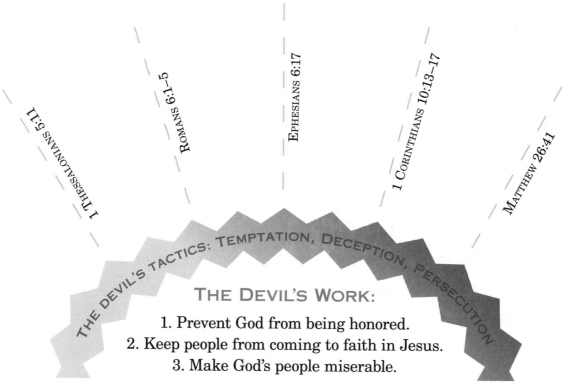

1 THESSALONIANS 5:11

ROMANS 6:1–5

EPHESIANS 6:17

1 CORINTHIANS 10:13–17

MATTHEW 26:41

THE DEVIL'S TACTICS: TEMPTATION, DECEPTION, PERSECUTION

THE DEVIL'S WORK:

1. Prevent God from being honored.
2. Keep people from coming to faith in Jesus.
3. Make God's people miserable.

Review

Satan: The chief of the fallen angels; created holy, he became evil and rebelled against God. The name *Satan* means "adversary." He is the enemy of God and God's people.

Devil: Another name for Satan; this name means "slanderer" or "accuser." Satan tries to torment us by reminding us of our sins, blaming us, and speaking against God and God's mercy. (See Zechariah 3:1–5; Revelation 12:9.) Because of Jesus' death on the cross, our heavenly Father no longer listens to Satan's accusations.

Demons: Evil angels; a name for the angels who joined Satan when he rebelled against God.

The Battle Continues

Suppose you could capture the battle plan Satan and his demons want to use against you. What would it look like? Maybe it would be something like the strategy on the paper below. How might you counter each ploy?

Lucifer's Top Ten Tempting Techniques

1. Tell Christians that disobeying God is not so bad. Tell them He won't care as long as it's just a little thing and they don't do it too often.

2. Once they sin, turn on them and make them feel guilty and afraid. Tell them God can't possibly forgive them.

3. Say, over and over again, "Everybody's doing it. You'll be left out if you don't."

4. Convince them that what their friends think is more important than what God thinks.

5. Talk them into believing everybody will laugh at them for trying to be so good and holy.

6. Talk them out of going to their moms, dads, teachers, or pastors when they have a problem.

7. Get them to think what they see on television and in the movies is how everybody really lives.

8. Tell them again and again about terrible things that could happen so that they worry and forget Jesus' promises to be with them.

9. Get their best friends on your side and use them as your helpers. Temptations from friends are harder for kids to resist.

10. Whatever you do, keep them from reading the Bible! Keep them from remembering Jesus' promises to forgive them and to bless them through Baptism and the Lord's Supper!

Remember

"Be strong _____ and in the strength of His might. Put on the whole armor of God, that you may be able to stand against _____ of the devil." (Ephesians 6:10–11)

Are heaven and hell real places?

"Be Afraid! Be Very Afraid!"

WHY ARE SO MANY PEOPLE AFRAID TO DIE?

_____

_____

WHY IS DEATH NOT FEARFUL TO CHRISTIANS? SEE ECCLESIASTES 12:7; LUKE 23:42–43.

_____

_____

WHY ARE SO MANY PEOPLE AFRAID OF JUDGMENT DAY?

Genesis 6:5–6: "The LORD saw that the wickedness of man was great in the earth, and that every intention of the thoughts of his heart was only evil continually. And the LORD was sorry that He had made man on the earth, and it grieved Him to His heart."

2 Peter 2:4–6: "God did not spare angels when they sinned, but cast them into hell and committed them to chains of gloomy darkness. . . . He did not spare the ancient world . . . when He brought a flood upon the world of the ungodly; . . . turning the cities of Sodom and Gomorrah to ashes He condemned them to extinction, making them an example of what is going to happen to the ungodly."

WHY DON'T CHRISTIANS NEED TO FEAR JUDGMENT DAY? READ ROMANS 10:9.

_____

_____

Review

Inherit: To receive a gift from the estate of someone who has died. One can inherit money, property, jewelry, or something intangible. _Example:_ I inherited a wooden rolltop desk and a sense of humor from my grandpa.

Can You Pass the Judgment Day Test?
(See Matthew 25:31–46.)

(A.) God gives you _____ (2 Corinthians 5:10, 19, 21)

(B.) God gives you _____ (1 John 4:17)

(C.) God gives you _____ (1 Corinthians 15:57)

(D.) God gives you _____ (1 Thessalonians 4:16–18)

God's Ultimate Protection

"[God] defends me against all danger
and guards and protects me from all evil."

From the Explanation of the First Article of the Apostles' Creed

Read Revelation 21, highlighting words that describe what heaven is like. Then celebrate these words of Jesus to all believers in Him: "Rejoice that your names are written in heaven" (Luke 10:20b).

God gets us there _____.

God keeps us there _____.

Remember

"According to [God's] great mercy,
He has caused us to be born again to a living hope
through the resurrection of Jesus Christ from the dead,
to an inheritance that is imperishable, undefiled, and unfading,
kept in heaven for you." (1 Peter 1:3–4)

What makes people so special, anyway?

We Are God's Handiwork

Directions: Read the Bible references and then tell in what unique ways God demonstrated His special love and care for human beings.

Genesis 2:7

_____

_____

1 Peter 2:24

_____

_____

Isaiah 41:10, 13

_____

_____

PSALM 8:1, 3–6, 9

O LORD, our Lord,
  how majestic is Your name in all the earth!
You have set Your glory above the heavens. . . .
When I look at Your heavens, the work of Your fingers,
  the moon and the stars, which You have set in place,
what is man that You are mindful of him,
  and the son of man that You care for him?
Yet You have made him a little lower than the heavenly beings
  and crowned him with glory and honor.
You have given him dominion over the works of Your hands;
  You have put all things under his feet . . .
O LORD, our Lord,
  how majestic is Your name in all the earth!

Review

Image: God's likeness placed in humans, gifting them with reasoning ability and many other attributes so that they can relate to God and live as caretakers of His world.

Soul: The breath of life from God that gives the rational, immortal spirit by which humans are distinguished from animals.

Holy: Set apart for a sacred purpose; pure; without sin.

In God's Image

Draw a line from each question to a picture that answers it.

1. Who can use intellectual reasoning?
   (Determine mathematically how to divide a large group into five smaller groups.)

2. Who can choose, plan, and imagine?
   (Create a picture of something you hope to do in heaven.)

3. Who can invent?
   (Invent a new song or symbol that praises the Lord.)

4. Who can have faith in what is not seen?
   (Write a poem that speaks of your trust in Jesus.)

5. Who can record information for future reference?
   (Write a favorite Bible verse on a piece of colored paper.)

6. Who can spiritually recognize the true God?
   (Say together the Apostles' Creed.)

Restored!

Heaven will be a place of perfect peace and joy, where we will live as God intended for His people and His creation. Read Isaiah 11:6–10. Draw lines to match up the pairs that will live in peace.

baby calf	little lamb	infant child	cow	young goat

spotted leopard	lion	bear	cobra snake	wolf

Remember

"By grace you have been saved through faith. And this is not your own doing; it is the gift of God, not a result of works, so that no one may boast. For we are His workmanship, created in Christ Jesus for good works."

(Ephesians 2:8–10)

How do we use what God has given us?

What If?

In your small group, brainstorm as many ideas as you can think of about what you could do in the following situations. Write down the ideas in the boxes. Then select one person to share your thoughts with the rest of the class.

1. What if you won a case of one thousand pencils?

2. What if your family received thirty-two quarts of strawberries?

3. What if you cleaned your bedroom closet and found twenty-five toys that you no longer want?

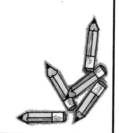

4. What if you had one hundred dollars and there was nothing you needed or wanted to spend it on?

5. What if you had plenty of time with nothing to do on a Saturday afternoon?

6. What if you had some really good news?

Review

Abundance (abundant, abundantly): More than enough; more than we need.

Good stewardship: Managing someone else's property or possessions wisely and well.

Abundant Gifts

"All this He does only out of fatherly, divine goodness and mercy, without any merit or worthiness in me." (From the explanation of the First Article of the Apostles' Creed)

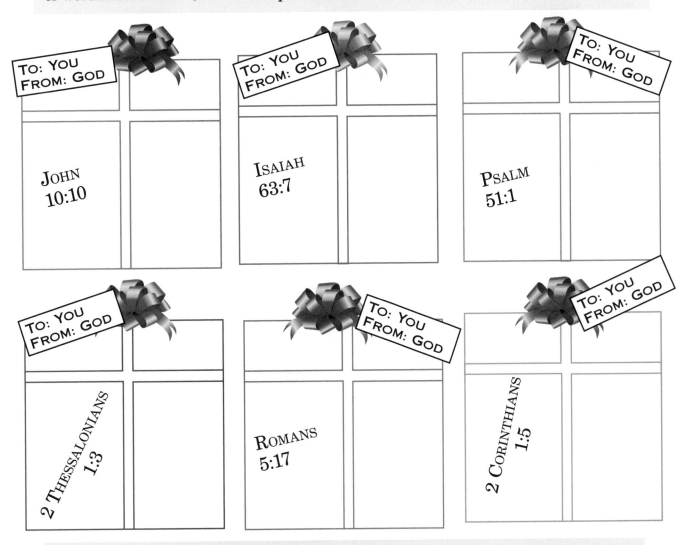

TO: YOU FROM: GOD — JOHN 10:10

TO: YOU FROM: GOD — ISAIAH 63:7

TO: YOU FROM: GOD — PSALM 51:1

TO: YOU FROM: GOD — 2 THESSALONIANS 1:3

TO: YOU FROM: GOD — ROMANS 5:17

TO: YOU FROM: GOD — 2 CORINTHIANS 1:5

What is our response to God's abundant blessings?

Overflowing _____ (2 Corinthians 7:4).

Overflowing _____ (2 Corinthians 9:12).

"For all this it is my duty to thank and praise, serve and obey Him. This is most certainly true." *(From the explanation of the First Article of the Apostles' Creed)*

Remember

"Whatever you do, in word or deed, do everything in the name of the Lord Jesus, giving thanks to God the Father through Him."

(Colossians 3:17)

How does God protect us?

Fearometer

Think about the average person your age. Name ten common fears people in fifth grade face. Print each fear along a vertical line at the bottom of the graph. Next, think about how strong each fear you've named is in the mind of a typical fifth grader. Use a different color of crayon or colored pencil to graph the level of concern for each fear on the Fearometer.

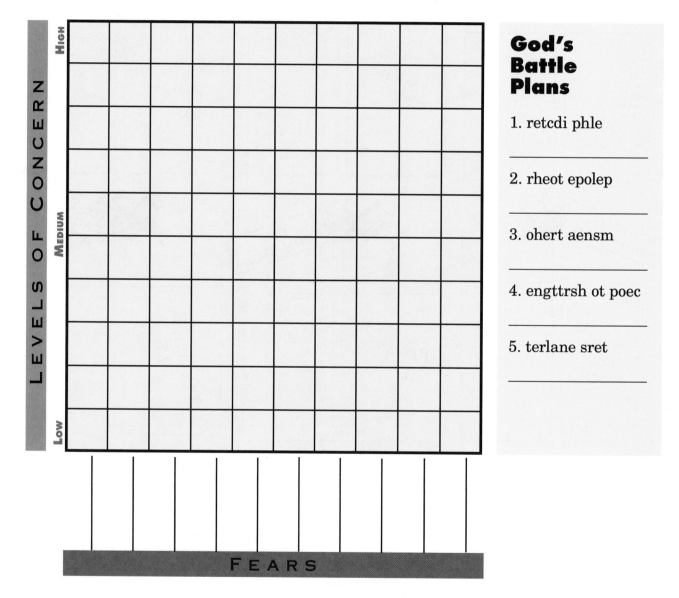

LEVELS OF CONCERN

HIGH

MEDIUM

LOW

FEARS

God's Battle Plans

1. retcdi phle

_____

2. rheot epolep

_____

3. ohert aensm

_____

4. engttrsh ot poec

_____

5. terlane sret

_____

Review

Place these words with their definitions: **fear, shield, trust.**

1. to defend _____

2. to be afraid _____

3. to protect _____

4. to have confidence _____

5. to honor and respect _____

6. to be certain _____

Blessed Even When Troubled

We know that for those who love God all things work together for good. . . . Who shall separate us from the love of Christ? Shall tribulation, or distress, or persecution, or famine? . . . No, in all these things we are more than conquerors through Him who loved us. For I am sure that neither death nor life, nor angels nor rulers, nor things present nor things to come, nor powers, nor height nor depth, nor anything else in all creation, will be able to separate us from the love of God in Christ Jesus our Lord.

(Romans 8:28, 35, 37–39)

Listed below are some circumstances that may cause trouble and fear in our lives. As you read each trouble, think about God's promise in Romans 8. How can God's love for us in Jesus bring a blessing even when we are having troubles? (Also read more of God's promises in Psalm 91:15–16.)

Troubles

God Continues to Bless Us

A failing grade

A long-term illness

Devastating storms

Unkind people

Remember

"You are my hiding place and my shield; I hope in Your word."

(Psalm 119:114)

Why does God bless us?

> "All this He does only out of fatherly, divine goodness and mercy,
> without any merit or worthiness in me."
>
> *(Luther's Small Catechism, explanation of the First Article of the Apostles' Creed)*

How Long?

How long you would search for each of the following lost items? Draw a line from each item to the place on the continuum line.

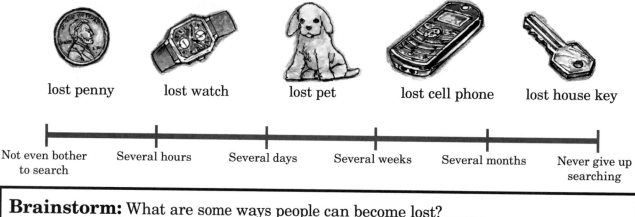

| lost penny | lost watch | lost pet | lost cell phone | lost house key |

Not even bother to search — Several hours — Several days — Several weeks — Several months — Never give up searching

---

Brainstorm: What are some ways people can become lost? _____

_____

_____

Riddle: Who am I? I need someone to take care of me because I am vulnerable and often get into trouble. I get lost and have no idea how to get back to a safe place. Often I am not even aware of the dangers around me. Sometimes I blindly follow others, even when it's the wrong way to go. **Who am I?** _____

Riddle: Who am I? I know all of your names. I know what you need and where you need to go. If you get in danger or go the wrong way, I find you and lead you back where you belong. I'm always with you. I would even risk my life for you. **Who am I?**

_____

Review

With your teacher's help, draw lines to match the Greek words for various kinds of love with their definitions.

1. agape   a. to like something. *I love chocolate cake.*

2. eros   b. kind, caring, unselfish affection. *She loves her friends and family.*

3. filial   c. romantic love. *My brother says he loves his girlfriend.*

4. ??   d. unconditional and undeserved love. *God wants us to share His love with others.*

The Love of the Good Shepherd

Directions: Highlight each verb or verb phrase in Psalm 23 that tells of something our Lord does for you. Then answer the questions on the right.

Psalm 23

The LORD is my shepherd;
    I shall not want.
He makes me lie down
    in green pastures.
He leads me beside still
    waters.
He restores my soul.
He leads me in paths of
    righteousness for His
    name's sake.

Even though I walk through
    the valley of the shadow of death,
    I will fear no evil,
for You are with me;
    Your rod and Your staff,
    they comfort me.

You prepare a table before me
    in the presence of my enemies;
You anoint my head with oil;
    my cup overflows.
Surely goodness and mercy shall
    follow me
    all the days of my life,
and I shall dwell in the house of
    the LORD forever.

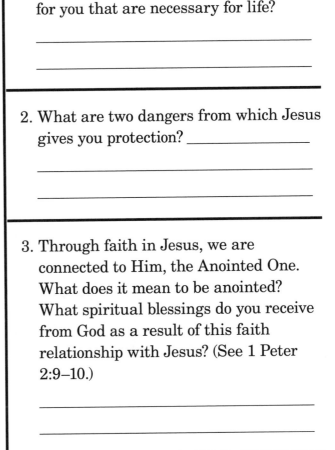

1. What are three things Jesus provides for you that are necessary for life?

  _____

  _____

2. What are two dangers from which Jesus gives you protection? _____

  _____

  _____

3. Through faith in Jesus, we are connected to Him, the Anointed One. What does it mean to be anointed? What spiritual blessings do you receive from God as a result of this faith relationship with Jesus? (See 1 Peter 2:9–10.)

  _____

  _____

4. Why can you be certain that you belong to Jesus, our Good Shepherd, forever? (See John 10:27–28.)

  _____

  _____

Remember

"Therefore be imitators of God, as beloved children. And walk in love, as Christ loved us and gave Himself up for us, a fragrant offering and sacrifice to God." (Ephesians 5:1–2)

How do we offer back to God what He has given us?

For All This It Is My Duty

Work together to list ways that justified and sanctified children of God (that's you!) can respond lovingly to God's love.

THANK	PRAISE

SERVE	OBEY

Review

Pledge _____

Sacrifice _____

Covenant _____

_____

Stewardship _____

A Small Treasure

Change the title above to what you think Jesus would say.

Time (With a highlighter graph time you spend daily.)

Sleep				
School				
Eating				
Leisure				

(Hours)   0   6   12   18   24

Talents (List some of the things you do well.)

Good Stewardship

	USE WELL	SHARE WITH OTHERS	GLORIFY GOD

Remember

(Use five different colors to underline five responses to give to the Lord.)

"Make a joyful noise to the LORD, all the earth!

Serve the LORD with gladness!

Come into His presence with singing!"   (Psalm 100:1–2)

JESUS BRINGS SALVATION (SECOND ARTICLE)

Why is it important that Jesus is true God?

We Need Help

I want to draw and paint, but I can't! I would like help from

_____.

I want to sing like a star, but I can't! I would like help from

_____.

I want to toss a ball fast and hard, but I can't! I would like help from _____.

I want to be a comedian on TV, but I can't! I would like help from

_____.

I want to be holy and righteous, but I can't! I would like help from

_____.

We Really Need Help

"I DON'T CARE HOW INFLUENTIAL, CARING, OR SMART YOU GUYS ARE . . . WE ARE ALL GOING DOWN WITH THE SHIP!

Heaven Bound

Review

Find two meanings for the word *perish*. Look in the dictionary and also these Bible verses. One meaning is physical and the other is spiritual.

1. Perish (physically—Matthew 8:25) _____

2. Perish (spiritually—John 3:16) _____

Who can help with both of these? How? _____

We Need a . . .

- ❏ friend
- ❏ teacher
- ❏ good example
- ❏ nice guy

THAT'S NOT ENOUGH!

We Need Jesus in the Boat

God can:
1. Do miracles.
2. Send other people to help.
3. Provide ability to cope.
4. Give heavenly peace.

Storms of this life

Sin

Satan

Death

Remember

"And we know that for those who love God all things work together for good, for those who are called according to His purpose."

(Romans 8:28)

Why is it important that Jesus is true man?

Other gods

What some people think a god is:

Distant, doesn't care about us

Just a dreamlike, mystical idea

Made of metal or stone

Hurtful, scary, deceiving

What we know the true God is:

_____

_____

_____

_____

> The true God is t__t__lly r__ __l and p__rs__n__l.

When You Think about God . . .

What do these Scripture verses tell us about God?

John 14:6–10 _____

Job 19:25–27 _____

2 Corinthians 4:6 _____

Review

Jesus was not proud or pompous; He showed _____. Jesus was willing to be

_____—born poor, raised as a carpenter's son, misunderstood by many, mocked

and hated by many, and betrayed, denied, and deserted by His own friends. The greatest

_____ was death on a cross, because a cross was considered a curse.

God Incarnate

God is incomprehensible. So He became one of us, in the flesh (incarnate), so we can understand, relate, and approach God in Jesus. What are some of the ways Jesus humbled Himself? Describe or draw a picture.

Luke 2:7	Mark 10:43–45	Luke 23:33

Washed and Raised Up

A. What do we share with Jesus when we are washed in Baptism?

(Romans 6:3) _____

B. That's not the end of the story—what else do we share with Jesus in Baptism?

(Romans 6:4–5) _____

C. How can this be? Jesus _____ because He truly is a man, and Jesus _____ because He truly is God.

D. What does all of this mean for you and me? (Romans 6:11) _____

_____

Remember

"Christ Jesus, who, though He was in the form of God, did not count equality with God a thing to be grasped, but made Himself nothing, taking the form of a servant, being born in the likeness of men. And being found in human form, He humbled Himself by becoming obedient to the point of death, even death on a cross. Therefore God has highly exalted Him and bestowed on Him the name that is above every name, so that **at the name of Jesus every knee should bow, in heaven and on earth and under the earth, and every tongue confess that Jesus Christ is Lord,** to the glory of God the Father." (Philippians 2:5–11)

How does Jesus serve as my substitute?

Your Substitute

Put an X on the one that could take your place.

A	A	A	A
Table	Puppy	Person	Computer

What do these Bible verses tell about our substitute?

a. 2 Corinthians 8:9 _____

_____

_____

b. Philippians 2:5–7 _____

_____

_____

c. 2 Corinthians 5:21 _____

_____

_____

d. Romans 6:3–8 _____

_____

_____

Review

Sacrifice. In the blood sacrifices of the Old Testament, the lamb was the substitute for the people. When the lamb was sacrificed, its death carried the people's punishment for their sins. This ceremony prefigured the ultimate sacrifice of Jesus, the Lamb of God. Jesus was the ultimate substitute—true God and true man, holy and human. We live in New Testament times. Because of Jesus, there are no more blood sacrifices. Those ended with Jesus, the complete and perfect substitute. (See Hebrews 10:10, 14, 18.)

Why as a Baby?

a. Our Lord did not "lord it over all." What does that mean?

_____

_____

_____

b. What message did Jesus' humility give? _____

_____

_____

c. Identify another time when Jesus showed humility.

_____

_____

d. Explain in your own words what the symbol above tells you. _____

_____

_____

Why Go to So Much Trouble?

Why did God go to so much trouble, having His Son be born as one of us, only to later suffer and die on a cross? Why didn't He just snap His fingers and say, "Sin, be gone"? God wouldn't do that, because He is a just God. If there was no punishment for sin, the message would be "sin as much as you want because it doesn't matter anyway." This would not be justice from a just God. The penalty had to be paid. So God Himself took the punishment for us. He calls us to repentance and a new life in Christ.

Remember

"For our sake He made Him to be sin who knew no sin, so that in Him we might become the righteousness of God." (2 Corinthians 5:21)

Was Jesus a prophet or a prophecy?

J.B.—The Prophet Announced

Centuries before Jesus was born, Old Testament prophets announced that a prophet was coming to prepare people for the Messiah. The prophet Isaiah (40:3) said, "A voice cries, in the wilderness prepare the way of the LORD; make straight in the desert a highway for our God." Later, the prophet Malachi spoke this message from God: "Behold, I send My messenger, and he will prepare the way before Me" (Malachi 3:1). When that messenger, John, was born, his own father, Zechariah, prophesied: "And you, child, will be called the prophet of the Most High; for you will go before the Lord to prepare His ways, to give knowledge of salvation to His people in the forgiveness of their sins" (Luke 1:76–77). Why were Isaiah, Malachi, and Zechariah able to accurately foresee what would happen in the future? (See Luke 1:67.) _____

J.B.—The Prophet Announces

The prophet known as John the Baptist grew up to fulfill his role—he announced that Jesus, the Messiah, had finally come, and he told the people to prepare their hearts through repentance. What was John's message? Write his exact words from John 1:29: _____

_____

How were the people to prepare their hearts for the coming of the Savior? See Mark 1:4–8. _____

_____

Question 274 of *Luther's Small Catechism with Explanation* says, "Who are repentant believers? Repentant believers are those who are sorry for their sins (contrition) and believe in the Lord Jesus Christ as their Savior (faith)."

Review

Advent:	Something or someone is coming
Prophesy:	To tell what or who is coming
Prophet:	One who speaks a message from God (either a prediction, warning, or encouragement)

Jesus—The Prophet, the Message, the Fulfillment?

So which is it—prophet, message, or fulfillment? Actually, Jesus is all three!

A. **Jesus as the Prophet.** Jesus, as Prophet, not only spoke a message from God but He Himself is also _____. (See John 14:6–10.)

B. **Jesus as the message.** All of Scripture points to one message—the Messiah will save His people. So all of Scripture points to Jesus, because He is that Messiah Savior. (See John 5:39 and 1 Corinthians 15:3–4.)

C. **Jesus as the fulfillment.** Jesus completed all things for us. Every messianic prophecy came true in Him. (See Luke 24:44–45.)

JESUS IS THE WHOLE PACKAGE!

Are You a Prophet?

"What? Not me! I don't know what will happen in the future!" We often get caught up with the idea that a prophet predicts the future. Actually, that is not a necessary part of being a prophet. A true prophet speaks a message from God. Do you know any messages from God? The Bible is filled with God's messages! You are acting as a prophet whenever you tell someone the message of God's Word! Sometimes, biblical prophets warned the people about their sins or about an impending disaster; sometimes it was a message of encouragement. For example, listen to these words of encouragement in Isaiah 40:1–2: "Comfort, comfort My people, says your God. Speak tenderly to Jerusalem . . . that her iniquity is pardoned, that she has received from the LORD's hand double." What is important is that the message came from God.

Consider this situation: Your friend's mother was severely injured in a car accident and is in the hospital. What words of encouragement could you say to your friend—not words that are shallow wishes on a get-well card, not words of empty "happy psych"—but words you speak giving messages of hope from God and His Word.

_____

_____

Remember

"Long ago, at many times and in many ways, God spoke to our fathers by the _____, but in these last days He has spoken to us by His _____, whom He appointed the heir of all things, through whom also He created the world." Hebrews 1:1–2

How did Jesus serve as both priest and sacrifice?

Mediators

Chaylyn was a _____ for Lori and Sue. Chaylyn wanted to _____ the two girls so they would be friends again!

Sin separated us from God. Jesus is our _____. He died on the cross to _____ us to God.

Review

Reconciliation: Sin separated us from God. Jesus broke through that barrier and reconciled us to God when He died on the cross. Change the picture of the wall to a cross. Jesus has reconciled us with God once more. When God looks at us, He does not see sin. (Jesus has removed it.) When God looks at us, He sees righteousness (which Jesus gives to us). In God's eyes, we are now holy and blameless! (See Colossians 1:21–22.)

Priest? Sacrifice? Both?

OLD TESTAMENT

NEW TESTAMENT

PRIEST—MEDIATOR

PERFECT—COMPLETE
ONCE AND FOR ALL

What does each of these Bible verses teach about Jesus?

1. Hebrews 7:26 _____

2. Hebrews 9:11–12 _____

3. Hebrews 10:10 _____

4. Hebrews 10:18 _____

Who Is This Baby?

Mary and Joseph said

He is _____

_____.

(Matthew 1:21; Luke 2:21)

Simeon said this

baby is _____

_____.

(Luke 2:30–32)

Anna said

_____

through this baby.

(Luke 2:38)

I know this

baby is _____

_____.

Remember

"In Christ God was _____ the world to Himself, not counting their trespasses against them, and entrusting to us the message of _____." (2 Corinthians 5:19)

From what and for what did Jesus redeem us?

The Unexpected Gift

We often talk about Jesus as the "best Christmas gift." But He was not the gift people expected. They were looking for a mighty warrior and king. Read the Bible verses in the gift box to the right and list some of the unexpected things about Jesus.

Isaiah 55:8–9: "My thoughts are not your thoughts, neither are your ways My ways, declares the LORD. For as the heavens are higher than the earth, so are My ways higher than your ways and My thoughts than your thoughts."

1. Luke 2:11–12 _____

_____

2. John 1:45–46 _____

_____

3. Matthew 13:54–55 _____

4. Luke 19:7, 10 _____

_____

5. 1 Corinthians 1:23–25 _____

_____

6. Luke 24:1–11 _____

_____

The Redeemer

Instead of comparing Jesus our Redeemer to a gift box, perhaps it would help to compare Him to a gift certificate. (As our Redeemer, Jesus paid the price, purchasing us to buy us back.)

	PURCHASED FROM	PURCHASED WITH	PURCHASED FOR
Gift Certificate	fast-food place	money	lunch
My Redemption			

Review

Redeem: to buy back or to pay a debt owed by someone else. Jesus came to redeem Israel and all people from slavery to sin and death. We owe God perfect obedience, but we are sinners and cannot give Him what we owe. The penalty for our sin is death and separation from God. Jesus, our Redeemer, came to suffer that punishment in our place. He paid the price to set us free, not with money but with His own blood.

Is This the Christ?

Our Savior and Redeemer suffered and died on a cross for us. His enemies derided Him, and His followers felt hopeless; neither expected this could happen to the Promised One. But God's plan was perfect! Jesus did all things necessary to save us. Read Luke 23:32–47. Draw lines to connect the words to whoever said them.

"Father, forgive them, for they know not what they do."

"He saved others; let Him save Himself, if He is the Christ!"

"If you are the King of the Jews, save Yourself!"

"Father, into Your hands I commit My spirit!"

"Are You not the Christ? Save Yourself and us!"

"Certainly this man was innocent!"

"This is the King of the Jews."

"Jesus, remember me when You come into Your kingdom."

"Truly, I say to you, today you will be with Me in Paradise."

Remember

" I have _____ your transgressions like a cloud and your _____ like mist; return to Me, for I have _____ you." (Isaiah 44:22)

What does Jesus' resurrection as the Lord of Life mean for us?

The Christmas–Easter Connection

Without Easter, the Christmas story would be just that—a sweet story. Scripture says, "If Christ has not been raised, your faith is futile and you are still in your sins" (1 Corinthians 15:17). Easter completes God's plan of salvation begun in Christ at Christmas. Read this poem to find other Christmas–Easter connections.

Along with the manger, let's look at the cross.
Christ's birth is just part of the story.
He suffered and died to remove all our sins.
So praise God and give Him the glory!

A tree may be covered with ornaments bright.
A tree may serve purposes lowly.
The wood of a tree built a manger so small
And a cross for our Savior most holy.

A beautiful star shining bright in the sky
Announced that the Savior is here.
The star points remind us of five of His wounds
From the hard-driven nails and a spear.

The angels rejoiced and they sang of God's peace
As they told that the Savior was born.
And angels proclaimed, "He's alive as He said,"
As Christ rose on that bright Easter morn.

—csb

Review

State of Humiliation: Christ's humiliation was that as man He did not always or fully use His divine powers. (Read Philippians 2:5–8.)

State of Exaltation: Christ's exaltation is that as man He now fully and always uses His divine powers. (Read Philippians 2:9–11.)

(Adapted from Luther's Small Catechism with Explanation)

Another Unexpected Gift

Just as the Savior born as a baby in Bethlehem was unexpected by many people, the Savior rising from death to life at Easter surprised many people (even though the Lord had foretold both). This event brings us the gift Jesus described when He said, "Because I live, you also will live" (John 14:19). Match the following statements with the related, supporting Bible verses.

1. The Old Testament said this would happen.   a. Mark 16:9–11

2. Jesus Himself said He would rise from the dead.   b. Hebrews 11:1

3. Even the witness of friends did not convince everyone.   c. Job 19:25–27

4. Jesus appeared alive to remove all doubt and uncertainty. d. John 20:29

5. We believe His resurrection by faith.   e. Matthew 16:21

6. Jesus gives a special blessing to you and me.   f. John 20:24–28

A New Kind of Heartburn

Television commercials often speak of medicines to take to get relief from the pain of indigestion—upset stomach, which is also called *heartburn*. Today's Bible story speaks of a different type of *burning heart*. In Luke 24:32, the disciples were excited to learn of the relief Jesus brought through His death and resurrection. Complete this acrostic with words and phrases that tell of the blessings of Easter that *burn in our hearts*.

R _____

E _____

L _____

I _____

E _____

F _____

Remember

"Now faith is the _____ of things hoped for, the _____ of things not seen." (Hebrews 11:1)

What is the purpose of the second coming of Jesus as King of kings?

The Advent of Our King

PAST: JESUS CAME	PRESENT: JESUS COMES	FUTURE: JESUS WILL COME

Once He Came in Blessing

1. Once He came in blessing,
   All our sins redressing;
   Came in likeness lowly,
   Son of God most holy;
   Bore the cross to save us;
   Hope and freedom gave us.

2. Now He gently leads us;
   With Himself He feeds us
   Precious food from heaven,
   Pledge of peace here given,
   Manna that will nourish
   Souls that they may flourish.

3. Soon will come that hour
   When with mighty power
   Christ will come in splendor
   And will judgment render,
   With the faithful sharing
   Joy beyond comparing.

4. Come, then, O Lord Jesus,
   From our sins release us.
   Keep our hearts believing,
   That we, grace receiving,
   Ever may confess You
   Till in heav'n we bless You.

(Lutheran Service Book 333)

Second Coming—Last Day—Judgment Day—Christ's Return

_____

(The words above all refer to the same event. Write what you know about that day.)

King of Kings

Why did they want to find the King?

_____
_____
_____
_____

Matthew 2:1–2, 10–11

Why did they want to make Jesus King?

_____
_____
_____
_____

John 6:10-11, 14-17

Why did they crown Jesus as King?

_____
_____
_____

Matthew 27:27-31

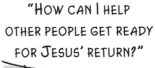

Where will Jesus rule eternally as King?

_____
_____
_____

Matthew 25:31, 34

Urgent! The End Is Near!

"I THINK JUDGMENT DAY SOUNDS SCARY!"

"CAN I BE CERTAIN JESUS WILL RETURN AND TAKE ME TO HEAVEN?"

"HOW CAN I PREPARE RIGHT NOW FOR THE LAST DAY?"

"HOW CAN I HELP OTHER PEOPLE GET READY FOR JESUS' RETURN?"

Remember

[Jesus says:] "Surely I am coming soon."

[We reply:] "Amen. Come, Lord Jesus!" (Revelation 22:20)

What do other names of Jesus tell about who He is?

What's in a Name?

Match these meanings with the biblical names:

Star	My God's Promise	Beloved	Gift of God	God Will Increase
Rock	God Gives Grace	Listens	Courageous	Father of Multitude
Earth	Saved from Water	Deceiver	Laughter	Kind Friend

1. Adam __ __ __ __ __

2. Abraham __ __ __ __ __ __ __ __ __ __ __ __ __ __ __ __ __

3. Isaac __ __ __ __ __ __ __

4. Jacob __ __ __ __ __ __ __

5. Joseph __ __ __ __ __ __ __ __ __ __ __ __ __ __

6. Moses __ __ __ __ __ __ __ __ __ __ __ __ __

7. Ruth __ __ __ __ __ __ __ __ __

8. Samuel __ __ __ __ __ __ __

9. David __ __ __ __ __ __

10. Esther __ __ __ __

11. Elizabeth __ __ __ __ __ __ __ __ __ __ __ __ __ __

12. Andrew __ __ __ __ __ __ __ __ __

13. Matthew __ __ __ __ __ __ __ __ __ __

14. John __ __ __ __ __ __ __ __ __ __ __ __ __

15. Peter __ __ __ __

Now look at the four names of Jesus in the Word Study box below. How do those names tell us who Jesus is? _____

Review

Draw lines to match names and meanings.

Christ   a. Greek form of Jeshua: "the Lord saves"

Messiah   b. Hebrew for "anointed"

Immanuel   c. Greek for "Messiah"

Jesus   d. Hebrew for "God with us"

That's My Name — Use It Often

There are over one hundred names for Jesus in the Bible. Complete these "birth certificates" by explaining the significance of the name listed.

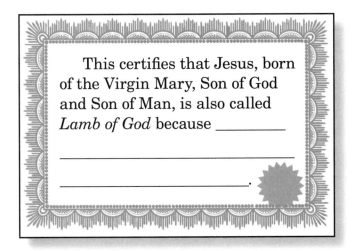

This certifies that Jesus, born of the Virgin Mary, Son of God and Son of Man, is also called *Lamb of God* because _____ _____ _____ .

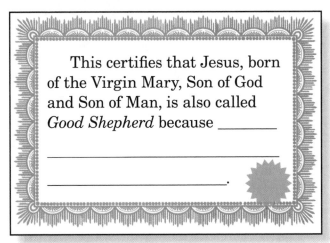

This certifies that Jesus, born of the Virgin Mary, Son of God and Son of Man, is also called *Good Shepherd* because _____ _____ _____ .

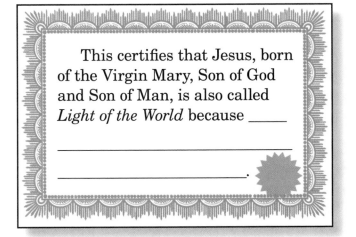

This certifies that Jesus, born of the Virgin Mary, Son of God and Son of Man, is also called *Light of the World* because _____ _____ _____ .

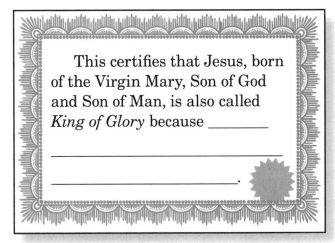

This certifies that Jesus, born of the Virgin Mary, Son of God and Son of Man, is also called *King of Glory* because _____ _____ _____ .

Name Above All Names

Choose one or more of the many names of Jesus that are particularly meaningful to you and use them in a prayer: _____

_____

Remember

"Therefore God has highly exalted Him and bestowed on Him the name that is above every name, so that at the name of Jesus every knee should bow, in heaven and on earth and under the earth, and every tongue confess that Jesus Christ is Lord." (Philippians 2: 9–11)

What names do we now have in Christ, and what does this mean for our lives?

What's in a Name—Part 2

A name can identify you, telling about these traits:

	YOUR FAMILY	WHERE YOU ARE FROM	WHO/WHAT YOU BELONG TO
Example:	I'm a Robertson	I'm a Texan	I'm a New York Yankees fan
Yourself:			

Identify these important names. Circle each one that applies to you.

A. Acts 11:26 _____   B. 1 John 3:1 _____

C. Galatians 3:27 _____

"Clothing" Identification

Read Galatians 3:27 and Colossians 3:12–15 in the English Standard Version (ESV) and the New International Version (NIV). The ESV says to "put on Christ"; the NIV says to "clothe yourselves" (be covered) with Christ. If this is true in you, what do people identify or see in you? Write the words from Colossians 3:12–15 on the labels of the basketball shirts.

Review

Compassion—feeling the joy or sadness of someone else, leading to a positive response.

Persecution—mistreatment, verbal or physical assault, because of person's beliefs.

What Is That Aroma?

Each of these has an aroma (fragrance, smell) that surrounds you and fills the air. What aroma does God identify with us? (See 2 Corinthians 2:14–15.) _____ _____ When God looks at us, we don't have the "stink of sin" because we have _____. Jesus has removed the evil and surrounded us with His righteousness. What is this new redeemed life like? The explanation of the Second Article of the Apostles' Creed says "that I may be _____ _____ _____

Identify Them

WHO IS HE?

_____
_____
_____
_____
_____
_____
_____

WHO IS HE?

_____
_____
_____
_____
_____
_____
_____

Remember

"By this all people will know that you are My disciples, if you have love for one another." (John 13:35)

What does it mean to follow Jesus?

Twelve Who Followed

READ LUKE 5:1–11.

Where did the action take place? _____

_____

Whom did Jesus call? _____

_____

How did the men respond to Jesus' call? _____

_____

READ LUKE 5:27–32.

Where did the action take place? _____

_____

Whom did Jesus call? _____

_____

How did the man respond to Jesus' call? _____

_____

READ LUKE 6:12–16.

Where did the action take place? _____

_____

Whom did Jesus call? _____

_____

How did the men respond to Jesus' call? _____

_____

Review

Disciple: One who listens, understands, and follows the teachings and beliefs of another.
Christian discipleship: The actions of being a disciple: listening to, supporting, and living the ways and will of our Lord Jesus in faith.

Great Is God's Faithfulness

Read each Bible verse and summarize in a word or two God's action as He reaches down from heaven to guide and bless us.

"Though I walk in the midst of trouble, You preserve my life; You stretch out Your hand against the wrath of my enemies, and Your right hand delivers me." (Psalm 138:7)

"The eyes of all look to You, and You give them their food in due season. You open Your hand; You satisfy the desire of every living thing." (Psalm 145:15–16)

_____

_____

"He fulfills the desire of those who fear Him; He also hears their cry and saves them." (Psalm 145:19)

_____

"And we know that for those who love God all things work together for good, for those who are called according to His purpose." (Romans 8:28)

"Casting all your anxieties on Him, because He cares for you." (1 Peter 5:7)

_____

_____

Remember

"[Demand, Ask], and it will be given to you; [seek, sit], and you will find; [pound, knock], and it will be opened to you. For everyone who asks [loses, receives], and the one who seeks [finds, replaces], and to the one who knocks it will be [locked, opened]." (Matthew 7:7–8)

How is Jesus manifest in my life?

Manifested Faith

Follow your teacher's direction to fill in the blanks to complete each sentence below, giving background information on the account of Jesus healing the centurion's servant (Luke 7:1–10).

A centurion was a _____ in the Roman army. As his name implies, a centurion was in charge of _____ men. A centurion rose to his position of _____ through hard work and dedication. A centurion was a role model and a _____ for the men in his *centuria* (a group of one hundred soldiers). A centurion fought alongside his men in battle. His large plumed _____ helped his men to locate him on the battlefield. At the time of this lesson's Bible story, the _____ army occupied Israel. The army's presence often caused great irritation to the Israelites. But the centurion Jesus encountered was different. Let's find out more about him.

Faith Manifested in Me

In the space to the right, attach your photo (or a photocopy or picture you draw of yourself, or write your name there). On the lines below, write about words and actions in your life that show you are a disciple of Jesus. These things are part of who we are because we belong to God! We belong to God because Jesus has redeemed us and the Holy Spirit is working faith in our hearts and lives.

Review

Manifest *means* _____

_____

God Empowers Me to Share His Word

You know you are a disciple of Christ, but how do you know what to say when you have an opportunity to tell someone about Jesus' saving love? The Holy Spirit brings you to faith in Jesus and keeps you in faith in Him. The Holy Spirit helps you live as a disciple and share Jesus' love with others. The following seven Bible verses summarize the basic truth of God's saving grace. Read each verse, then fill in the blanks below to formulate an outline to use when sharing Jesus with others.

Bible Truth

1. "For God so loved the world, that He gave His only Son, that whoever believes in Him should not perish but have eternal life." (John 3:16)

2. "For all have sinned and fall short of the glory of God." (Romans 3:23)

3. "For the wages of sin is death, but the free gift of God is eternal life in Christ Jesus our Lord." (Romans 6:23)

4. "But God shows His love for us in that while we were still sinners, Christ died for us." (Romans 5:8)

5. "For I delivered to you as of first importance what I also received: that Christ died for our sins in accordance with the Scriptures, that He was buried, that He was raised on the third day in accordance with the Scriptures." (1 Corinthians 15:3–4)

6. "Then he brought them out and said, 'Sirs, what must I do to be saved?' And they said, 'Believe in the Lord Jesus, and you will be saved, you and your household.' " (Acts 16:30–31)

7. "For by grace you have been saved through faith. And this is not your own doing; it is the gift of God, not a result of works, so that no one may boast." (Ephesians 2:8–9)

Sharing Outline

1. God _____ you!

2. You are a _____.

3. God punishes _____.

4. _____ took our punishment.

5. Jesus _____ from the dead.

6. Jesus offers _____ of sins and eternal _____ to those who believe in Him.

7. Salvation is a _____ _____ from God.

Adapted from "Salvation Outline," *Luther's Small Catechism with Explanation* (St. Louis: CPH, 1986, 1991), p. 258.

Remember

"So Jesus said to the Jews who had believed in Him, 'If you _____ in My word, you are truly My _____, and you will know the _____, and the _____ will set you free.' " (John 8:31–32)

Is discipleship passive or active?

Challenge and Change

Read each description below. Match it with the person it identifies.

1. _____ Despite failing the sixth grade, this famous statesman captured the attention of millions during World War II with inspiring speeches.

2. _____ Despite being blind and deaf due to an illness as a young child, this woman went on to graduate college and become a world-famous speaker and author.

3. _____ Born to an undistinguished family, this person moved often with his father, sister, and brother. He was once kicked in the head by a horse and thought to be dead. He attended school for a very short period of time. He became a good debater, thinker, and leader.

4. _____ When he was a boy, his teacher told him he was too stupid to learn anything. During his life, this inventor earned 1093 patents.

5. _____ His music teacher called him hopeless as a composer. He wrote some of his greatest music while completely deaf.

A. Thomas Edison

B. Ludwig van Beethoven

C. Abraham Lincoln

D. Winston Churchill

E. Helen Keller

Consider a challenge you want to overcome. Pray to the Lord to help you meet the challenge according to His will and timing.

Debby, Mo, and Zach

God often makes unexpected and unusual choices in people—and then He changes things!

What was unexpected about Deborah? See Judges 4:4–10. _____

_____

What was unusual about God's choice of Moses as a leader? See Exodus 2:11–15. _____

_____

Why does God make such unexpected choices? See 1 Corinthians 1:25–27. _____

_____

"But I'm just a kid! Can God use me?" See 1 Timothy 4:12. _____

_____

Let's learn about the great change God made in Zacchaeus, turning a cheat, liar, and traitor into a believer, follower, and disciple. See Luke 19:1–10.

Review

Conversion: *A change, turn around, transformation, new life in Christ.*

Discipleship Power

We are hopeless sinners without God. However, His amazing INPUT changes and transforms us so that we can live for Him. That is our OUTPUT. Write examples of this INPUT and OUTPUT after hearing the related Bible verses.

Discipleship: Passive, Active, and Proactive

Passive sin is not doing what you should do. Active sin is doing what you should not do. God changes our lives, and now we are His disciples. Brainstorm passive, active, and even proactive ways we can live a live of faith (discipleship). *Proactive* means doing something positive ahead of time, in advance, before you are asked or before help is needed.

PASSIVE	ACTIVE	PROACTIVE

Remember

"Create in me a clean heart, O God, and renew a right spirit within me. Cast me not away from Your presence, and take not Your Holy Spirit from me. Restore to me the joy of Your salvation, and uphold me with a willing spirit." (Psalm 51:10–12)

Discipleship:
In what ways can I be a disciple, now and in the future?

God's Many Disciples

Match these followers of Jesus with their worldly jobs or duties.

1. Moses _____
2. David _____
3. Peter _____
4. Matthew _____

5. Lydia _____
6. Paul _____
7. Cornelius _____
8. Deborah _____

9. Luke _____
10. Joseph (NT) _____
11. Tabitha (Dorcas) _____
12. Joseph (OT) _____

a. tentmaker
b. physician
c. seller of purple cloth

d. carpenter
e. judge
f. seamstress

g. shepherd
h. Roman centurion
i. shepherd

j. fisherman
k. tax collector
l. slave

God Opened Her Heart

God used the apostle Paul to bring the Gospel to Lydia and her friends and family. Lydia sold purple cloth, which was very expensive in those days. Her clients were wealthy, and she herself was probably rich. But aside from her vocation, she found a new calling as a disciple of Christ. Look at the map below to see the setting of this Bible narrative in Acts 16:11–15.

Review

Vocation: A person's career or occupation.

Calling: A strong inner desire toward a particular course of action. (A person's calling is often fulfilled in his or her chosen profession or vocation.)

Vocations and Callings

Write ways each of these people can show discipleship (a calling to serve the Lord) in each of these vocations.

_____

_____

_____

_____

_____

_____

_____

_____

_____

_____

_____

_____

_____

_____

_____

_____

Remember

"Whatever you do, work heartily, as for the _____ and not for men, knowing that from the _____ you will receive the inheritance as your reward. You are serving the _____ Christ." (Colossians 3:23–24)

109

Prayer: Who? Where? What? When? Why?

No Prayer Rules?

God does not have rules about the way we pray, but He does expect this of all believers:

A. See Matthew 21:22: TRUST _____.

B. See James 1:6–7: TRUST _____.

C. See 1 John 5:14: TRUST _____.

Questions about Prayer

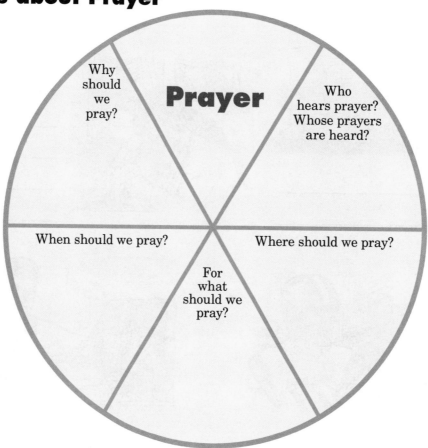

Review

Hypocrite: A person who pretends to be something he or she is not; false appearance. (Let God be the judge of people's hearts. Do not make judgments yourself, especially in matters in which the person was not being deceptive. For example, if a person does wrong to you by forgetting or failing to help, but not by intention or deceit, do not judge him or her. Leave such judgments to the Lord.)

Prayer Guidelines

Write a short sentence that is an example of each type of prayer.

CONFESSION: admitting what you've done wrong.   [   ]

_____

ADORATION: praising God for His greatness.   [   ]

_____

SUPPLICATION: asking for wants and needs.   [   ]

_____

THANKSGIVING: identifying and appreciating blessings.   [   ]

_____

What If I Don't Know What to Say?

"The Spirit helps us in our weakness. For we do not know what to pray for as we ought, but the Spirit Himself intercedes for us with groaning too deep for words." (Romans 8:26)

Remember

"Let the words of my mouth and the meditation of my heart be acceptable in Your sight, O Lord, my rock and my redeemer."

(Psalm 19:14)

To whom should we pray?

Who? Where? What? When? Why?

The Introduction. **Our Father who art in heaven.** *What does this mean?* With these words God tenderly invites us to believe that He is our true Father and that we are His true children, so that with all boldness and confidence we may ask Him as dear children ask their dear father.

The First Petition. **Hallowed be Thy name.** *What does this mean?* God's name is certainly holy in itself, but we pray in this petition that it may be kept holy among us also. *How is God's name kept holy?* God's name is kept holy when the Word of God is taught in its truth and purity, and we, as the children of God, also lead holy lives according to it. Help us to do this, dear Father in heaven! But anyone who teaches or lives contrary to God's Word profanes the name of God among us. Protect us from this, heavenly Father!

God's Son

Jesus not only gave us the Lord's Prayer, but He also enables us to come to God to pray it. He gave us His righteousness (by exchanging it for our sins) so that we can be holy before our holy God. (Say or see 2 Corinthians 5:21.)

Because of Jesus, we have

—— —— —— —— —— —— —— —— —— ——.

(See Hebrews 4:16.)

Because of Jesus, God has

—— —— —— —— —— —— —— —— ——.

(See Psalm 103:13.)

Review

Petition: A request; asking for something.

Hallowed: (Clue) This is not a noun; it is an adjective.

Peter's Two Prayers

(Matthew 14:22–33)

PETER'S FIRST PRAYER

"Lord, if it is You, command me to come to You on the water."

Peter's Prayer

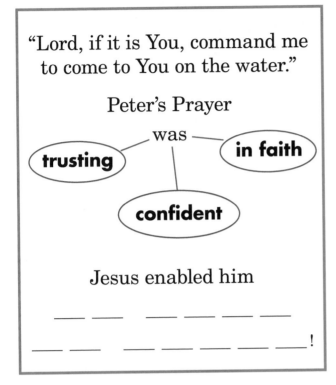

was — trusting — in faith — confident

Jesus enabled him

__ __ __   __ __ __ __

__ __   __ __ __ __ __ __!

PETER'S SECOND PRAYER

"Lord, save me."

What happened?

Peter took his eyes off Jesus.

Hebrews 12:2 NIV says to us, "Let us fix our eyes on Jesus." How do we do that? _____

_____

_____

_____

Keep His Name Holy

In this First Petition, we ask God to help us keep the Second and Third Commandments.

We do this when we

> __ __ __ __
> God's Word. (Isaiah 39:5)

> __ __ __ __
> God's Word. (Psalm 119:17)

Bless the LORD, O my soul, and all that is within me, bless His holy name! (Psalm 103:1)

Remember

"I will be a father to you, and you shall be sons and daughters to Me, says the Lord Almighty." (2 Corinthians 6:18)

Where should we pray?
(The Second and Third Petitions)

Whom Does God Want in His Kingdom?

Draw lines to connect the characters from the Bible with their descriptions.

1. Jacob	a. Coward
2. Gideon	b. Uneducated fishermen
3. Samson	c. Persecutor of Christians
4. Jeremiah	d. Liar
5. Peter, James, John	e. Traitor and tax collector
6. Matthew	f. Sad and depressed
7. Paul	g. Show-off

God thinks differently than people do. Look at 1 Samuel 16:6–13. God didn't look for the tallest, oldest, strongest, richest, or smartest person to be king. What did God look at?

_____

What does God want? (See 1 Timothy 2:3–4.) _____

"Thy Kingdom Come"

We belong to God—in His kingdom!

POWER　　　**GRACE**　　　**GLORY**

Review

Use a Bible dictionary or regular dictionary to find definitions.

Kingdom _____

Will _____

A Closer Look at the Kingdom

	Power	Grace	Glory
Can you see it?			
Where is it?			
What is God's action?			

"Thy Will Be Done"

1. "Dear God, help us win this game with a big score."

2. "Jenny is mean to me; make something bad happen to her."

3. "I pray that I will be very, very rich some day."

4. "Jesus, please make Grandma healthy again."

Remember

"For this is the will of My Father, that everyone who looks on the Son and believes in Him should have eternal life." (John 6:40)

For what should we pray?

God Meets Our Needs

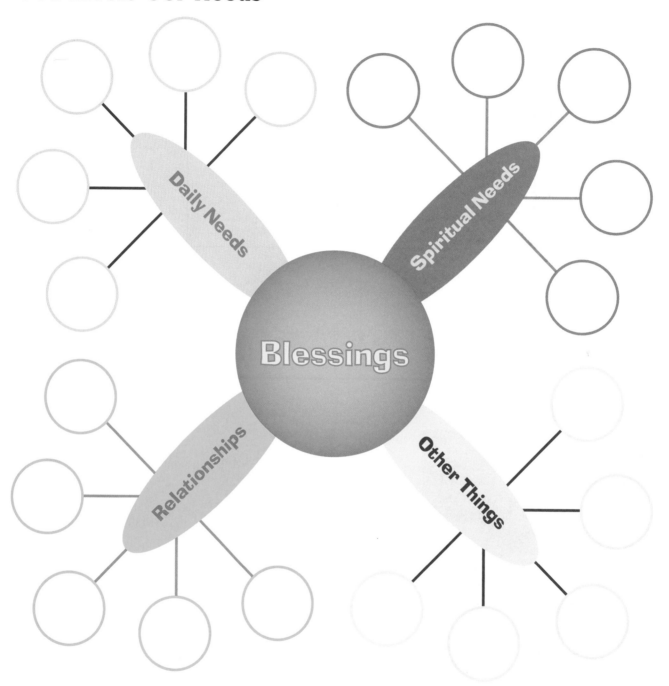

Review

Blessing: God blesses us with His good gifts; we bless Him with our thanks and praise. See Psalm 103:1–5.

Forgiveness: Through Christ, our wrongdoings are taken away and forgotten. We forgive others in thanksgiving of God's forgiveness. Forgive and forget!

Giving Thanks

Brainstorm ideas for giving thanks to God in these three ways. Put a check mark next to things you will do today or tomorrow.

PRAISING HIM FOR OUR BLESSINGS	TAKING CARE OF OUR BLESSINGS	SHARING OUR BLESSINGS WITH OTHERS

Remember

"Oh give thanks to the LORD, for He is good, for His steadfast love endures forever! Let the redeemed of the LORD say so." (Psalm 107:1–2)

When should we pray?

When You Have Troubles inside You (Temptations, Sin)

Some temptations are big and obvious, such as when someone is tempted to steal or murder. But the devil is very sneaky. He often uses simple things to tempt us to sin. How could each of these be a temptation to sin?

Laughter: _____

Math paper: _____

Bike ride: _____

A friend's suggestion: _____

A piece of candy: _____

The devil is clever and powerful. He eagerly attacks God's people, tempting them to sin. So what are we going to do? James 4:7–8 says, "Submit yourselves therefore to God. Resist the devil, and he will flee from you. Draw near to God, and He will draw near to you." 1 John 4:4 says, "He [Jesus] who is in you is greater than he [the devil] who is in the world."

When temptation comes your way, go to God in prayer and say,

"CHRIST, OUR LORD, LEAD US AWAY!"

When You Have Troubles around You (Evil in This World)

God's Actions for Our Problems

1. God can fix it.

2. God can bless us with people who help us with our problems.

3. God can help us adjust or cope with living with a problem.

4. Revelation 21:1–4.

Review

Environment: Surroundings, conditions, influences, or external factors that affect our lives.

An Amazing Story of an Amazing God Building Amazing Faith!

1. Read Acts 12:1–16. Peter was in jail. He had done nothing wrong. He could have been tempted to despair. What evidence do we have that Peter was not even worried about what was happening (vv. 6–7)? _____
_____

2. How could Peter sleep at a time when his life was threatened? _____
_____ (2 Corinthians 4:8–9 says, "We are afflicted in every way, but not crushed; perplexed, but not driven to despair; persecuted, but not forsaken.")

3. Peter was in jail because of the injustice and evil in the world around him! What was the reason Herod imprisoned Peter (vv. 1–3)? _____
_____

4. God intervened with a miracle this time! God can do miracles, but He doesn't always choose to do so. Sometimes He has another purpose in mind. What was God's purpose when Paul was jailed in Philippi (Acts 16:29–30)? _____
_____

5. God often works very quietly in our lives, but sometimes His answer to our prayers is absolutely amazing! What evidence do we have that the friends of Peter, who were praying for him, were totally surprised at God's answer to their prayers (vv. 13–16)?

_____

_____

_____

_____

_____

_____

_____

As Jesus taught us, we pray that God will "lead us not into temptation, but deliver us from evil." Don't be surprised at the way He answers you!

Remember

"The LORD will keep you from all evil; He will keep your life.
The LORD will keep your going out and your coming in
from this time forth and forevermore." (Psalm 121:7–8)

Why should we pray? (The Conclusion)

What Was the Question?

Why should we pray?
Because God <u>can</u> and <u>will</u> answer!

God's Answers:

YES _____

WAIT _____

NO _____

My Prayer

Write a prayer as an acrostic. Write your name in the boxes vertically (going down). Use each letter as the beginning letter of each line of your prayer.

☐ _____

☐ _____

☐ _____

☐ _____

☐ _____

☐ _____

☐ _____

☐ _____

☐ _____

☐ _____

☐ _____

☐ _____

Review

Spontaneous: ad-lib, automatic, free, impromptu, improvised, natural, off the top of my head, off-the-cuff, uncompelled, uncontrived, unplanned, unpremeditated, voluntary

The Steps of the Story

Use this outline to read about and discuss King Hezekiah's story in 2 Kings 19.

V. 1: Repentant and sad.

Vv. 2, 4b: Involved others in prayer.

V. 6: Received assurance.

V. 10: Was ridiculed and mocked.

V. 14: Presented the problem to the Lord.

V. 15: Began with praise.

Vv. 16, 19: Petitions: a problem and a request.

V. 20: God heard.

Vv. 32–35: God answered.

Simply Spontaneous!

A spontaneous prayer is one that comes to your heart and mind anywhere, often instantly, and often because you see something that reminds you of God and His care. It may be just a few words, and you can think them or say them. You don't have to ask for anything; simply thank God. He likes to hear what you are thinking. Just talk to God, and you are praying! Look at these pictures. Write a simple spontaneous prayer that you could pray about each thing pictured.

Remember

"Rejoice always, pray without ceasing, give thanks in all circumstances; for this is the will of God in Christ Jesus for you."

(1 Thessalonians 5:16–18)

Why do most of our worship services begin with Confession and Absolution?

Are You Ready for This?

Imagine that you pick up the mail on your way into the house when you get home from school this afternoon. Suppose you spot a letter addressed to you—from the White House in Washington DC! You open it and watch an invitation fall out. The president is inviting you to a dinner honoring the nation's young people. You

© Patricia Hofmeester/Shutterstock, Inc.

and fifteen others have been chosen to attend the dinner next week.

It's quite an honor! As you pack your suitcase, you'll probably think carefully about what to wear to the dinner. You probably won't consider your ragged T-shirt and stained gym shorts. Wearing them would insult the president and the other guests. It would even insult the nation! It would be disrespectful. Anyone who showed up dressed like that ought to be ashamed!

- How is meeting with God in worship like meeting the president? How is it different?

- When we come to worship our heavenly Father, He is concerned not about the condition of our clothes, but rather the condition of our hearts and lives. How can we honor and worship Him if we are covered with the spots and stains of sin? What kind of hearts and lives does He expect to see in those who come to worship Him?

- With that in mind, how would you answer this question: "Why do most of our worship services begin with Confession and Absolution?"

- Because of the Absolution we have through Jesus, what does God see now when He looks at us? See Colossians 1:22.

Review

Confession: To admit one's sins; to recognize what God says about our wrongdoing.

Absolution: An announcement or declaration of forgiveness.

Not Worthy

Jesus once told a story to illustrate what God's Absolution is like. Read it from Luke 15:11–24. Then match the elements of Jesus' story with their meaning.

1. The father in the parable

2. The son in the parable

3. The "reckless living" in "a far country" (v. 13)

4. The son's decision to ask to come home and work as a slave (v. 19)

5. The father watching for his son (v. 20)

6. The "best robe" (v. 22)

7. The "shoes" (v. 22)

8. The celebration (v. 23–24)

a. Slaves went barefoot; the father wanted to show his son belonged to the family. God takes us back as His own deeply-loved children.

b. Walking away from our heavenly Father to live in selfishness and disobedience.

c. The "robe of righteousness" Jesus earned for us on His cross.

d. Our heavenly Father won't force us to come back to Him, but He watches and waits eagerly for our return.

e. God, our heavenly Father.

f. The joy of God, the angels in heaven, other believers, and us ourselves.

g. Our idea that we can make up for our sins by what we do for God.

h. Each one of us, God's daughters and sons.

- When do you think the son in the story really repented—changed his mind and heart toward his sin and his father? (A) When he got hungry and decided to go home; (B) When he saw his father running toward him; (C) When the servants brought the robe, ring, and sandals; (D) At some other point.

- What brings you to true repentance most often?

Remember

"If we say we have no sin, we deceive ourselves, and the truth is not in us. If we confess our sins, He is faithful and just to forgive us our sin and to cleanse us from all unrighteousness." (1 John 1:8–9)

What sins do we confess and to whom?

Making Excuses or Confession?

When we sin, we can make excuses, or we can make confession. Put a check mark next to each excuse you've used at one time or another.

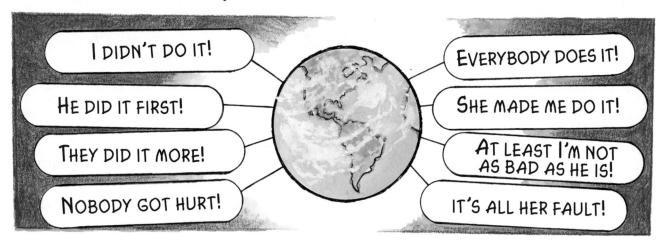

I DIDN'T DO IT!

HE DID IT FIRST!

THEY DID IT MORE!

NOBODY GOT HURT!

EVERYBODY DOES IT!

SHE MADE ME DO IT!

AT LEAST I'M NOT AS BAD AS HE IS!

IT'S ALL HER FAULT!

Did you grin a little sheepishly as you read the excuses above? We smile because we see ourselves in the list. Most of us have used every one of these excuses at one time or another. (Here's a secret that's not so secret: Adults often use these same excuses!)

Did you notice the exclamation marks behind each excuse? Much of the time, we know these excuses aren't exactly convincing. So we talk louder, trying to act more sure of ourselves.

Discuss these questions, being as honest as you can.

• When do kids your age use excuses like those above? Why? _____

_____

• When do adults use them? Why? _____

_____

• Why would people rather make excuses than make Confession? _____

_____

• Why does God want us to confess our sins to those we hurt? to Him? _____

_____

Review

Justified: To be declared guiltless or innocent; to be absolved of guilt.

Merciful: Characterized by compassion, pity, concern; the willingness to help someone in need, especially someone who doesn't deserve it.

The Pharisee and the Tax Collector

Much of what Jesus taught about sin and forgiveness took the form of parables. Last time, we explored the parable often called "The Lost Son" or "The Forgiving Father." As you read Luke 18:9–14, think about what title you might give this parable. Write two choices on the blanks below, and put a star next to the one you think fits best. Keep in mind that a good title gives a summary of the main idea. _____

_____

Seeing My Sin/Seeing My Savior

The Pharisee was too proud to realize his own sin. He had fooled himself. God gives us His Law as a gift to keep us from fooling ourselves into thinking—like the Pharisee—that God should be quite pleased with us, thank you very much. The Law helps us see our sin and our need for a Savior. (Seeing our sin would terrify us if it weren't for Jesus and the love He showed us on the cross!)

Christians have often thought about sin in different ways, creating different categories to help us understand God's Law more clearly. For example, "sins of commission" are sins we commit—times we actually do wrong. "Sins of omission" are good things we've omitted, times we fail to do what is right. See if you can list five sins of commission and five sins of omission in the spaces below.

Sins of Commission

1. _____
2. _____
3. _____
4. _____
5. _____

Sins of Omission

1. _____
2. _____
3. _____
4. _____
5. _____

Now go back over your lists. Put a **T** next to sins that are **Thoughts.** Put a **W** next to sins that are **Words.** Put an **A** next to sins that are **Actions.**

- Compare the lists you made with others in your class. What did you learn?
- When we confess our sins, we don't always remember (or even know about) all of them. Does God forgive the sins we don't remember? Explain.
- Jesus says the tax collector went home "justified." How are you justified? (This is the most important question of all!)

Remember

> "**W**ho can discern his errors? Declare me innocent from hidden faults." (Psalm 19:12)

Who receives Absolution?

I'm Sorry (But Not Really)

Suppose you had a friend who hurt you in one way or another every day. Maybe you heard that person saying mean things about you behind your back twelve times. Maybe that person also lied to a teacher or the principal about you. Maybe you noticed things missing from your desk or locker and later saw those same things in your friend's backpack. Suppose that every time you talked to your friend about it, you got this reply: "Sorry!" After a while, those "sorrys" would probably get harder and harder to believe, wouldn't they? A "fake sorrow" is meaningless.

Does God believe our "sorrys"? Should He? Think about Confession, contrition, repentance, and forgiveness. Then, in the chart below, write down five to ten ways to tell the difference between a "true sorry" and a "fake sorry."

TRUE SORROW	FAKING IT

Review

Confession:	Admitting and stating accurately what you have done.
Contrition:	Sincere regret or sorrow for one's sins; remorse.
Repentance:	The change of heart and the renewed trust for God that leads to changed behaviors.
Restored:	As Jesus forgives us, we live new lives in repentance and faith.

Repentance in Corinth

(2 Corinthians 7:6–13)

The apostle Paul founded the church in Corinth. He lived with the believers there for eighteen months, telling many people about Jesus and making many friends. Finally, it was time to leave, to share the Gospel in other regions. Before long, though, Paul began receiving disturbing reports. The Corinthians were choosing up sides and quarreling with each other. Some felt so angry and hurt that they sued each other in court. They were showing disrespect for the Lord's Supper. Some were getting drunk and were breaking the Sixth Commandment. It was a mess. So Paul wrote a letter. He confronted them with their sins and told them they had to stop it. He sealed up the letter and sent it to Corinth. A friend carried Paul's letter to Corinth, and it took a long time to get there. For weeks, Paul prayed and wondered about how the Corinthians would respond. Would they get angry? Would they scoff and ignore him? Finally, Titus came back from a visit to Corinth. He brought news from the church there. Read about it here from 2 Corinthians 7.

To the church at Corinth:

God, who comforts the downcast, comforted us by the coming of Titus . . . as he told us of your longing, your mourning, your zeal. . . . For even if I made you grieve with my letter, I do not regret it. . . . As it is, I rejoice, not because you were grieved, but because you were grieved into repenting. For you felt a godly grief. . . . For godly grief produces a repentance that leads to salvation without regret, whereas worldly grief produces death. For see what earnestness this godly grief has produced in you. . . . Therefore we are comforted.

In Christ,
The apostle Paul

Remember

"Repent therefore, and turn again, that your sins may be blotted out, that times of refreshing may come from the presence of the Lord."

(Acts 3:19–20)

What is the Office of the Keys and the pastoral ministry?

Persecuted for Christ

The police shouted and pounded on the door. Pastor Uhorski (you-hor-ski) had been expecting them. World War II had ended a few months before. The Russian army had liberated Czechoslovakia from the Nazis—and then placed the nation under Communist rule. One by one, churches were closed and turned into museums and gyms.

Officials had visited Pastor Uhorski's home several times. "You can remain a pastor," they said slyly. "We don't mind. Just promise to tell us who comes each week to church. If you cooperate, we will take care of you."

But again and again, the young pastor refused. He would not betray his people. He paid for his courage with his freedom. The police imprisoned him and kept him in prison for over a decade.

The cell in which he lived for all those years was so small that he could stand in the

Photo: © 2010 David A. Fiala

middle, stretch out his arms, and touch the walls in all four directions. His captors beat him almost every day. Still, the young pastor would not give up his faith in Jesus or agree to betray the Christians he served.

Finally, afraid Pastor Uhorski was becoming famous as a martyr, the government "pardoned" him. In "recognition" for this pardon, he was sent to the Polish border to work in a coal mine. The person in charge of the mine sent him to the forests nearby to cut down trees to use as braces underground. Day by day, in cold and heat, snow and rain for forty years, Pastor Uhorski chopped wood. His hands grew calloused and his body weak. But every week in prison and in the forest, too, Pastor Uhorski wrote a new sermon.

Many Christians in the country of Slovakia today hold Pastor Uhorski in high esteem. Why is it so important that God's people have faithful pastors—in times of trouble and in times of peace?

Review

Esteem: To think highly of someone or something; to respect.

Office of the Keys: The authority Jesus gave to His Church here on earth to forgive the sins of those who repent and to refuse Absolution to the impenitent; congregations call pastors to use the Office of the Keys publicly on the congregation's behalf.

Training a Pastor
(2 Timothy 1:3–10; 3:14–17)

Today, pastors train for their work in schools called
"seminaries." The seminaries of the Lutheran Church Missouri Synod are in Fort Wayne, IN and St. Louis, MO and are pictured here.

Colleen M. Bartzsch, Concordia Theological Seminary

Photograph courtesy of Concordia Seminary, St. Louis.

At the time Jesus ascended to heaven, though, there were no seminaries. So how did pastors learn to care for God's people? And what does God ask of those He calls to serve as pastors? The Book of 2 Timothy gives us some clues. Read what the apostle Paul wrote to a young pastor named Timothy in 1:3–10 and 3:14–17. Then, on the lines below, write a summary of how God prepared Timothy to serve His people.

_____

_____

_____

_____

_____

My Pastor—A Gift that Keeps on Giving (the Gospel)

After reading 1 Thessalonians 5:11–18, discuss these questions as a group.

Q1. What does God expect your pastor to do for you? What does God expect you to do for your pastors?

Q2. Sadly, some Christians and churches end up fussing and fighting with each other and with their pastors. Why might this happen? What could we do if this would ever happen in our church?

Q3. How might you, your family, and your class encourage and support the pastor Jesus has given to you?

Remember

"**O**bey your leaders and submit to them, for they are keeping watch over your souls, as those who will have to give an account. Let them do this with joy and not with groaning, for that would be of no advantage to you." (Hebrews 13:17)

What is liturgical worship?

Liturgy—An Order of Worship

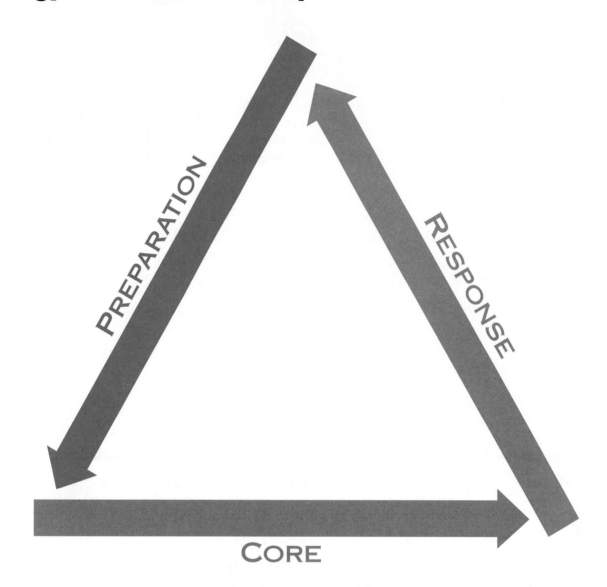

PREPARATION

RESPONSE

CORE

Review

Use the glossary to write the definition of each word.

Liturgy: _____

_____

Invocation: _____

Benediction: _____

A Common Order of Worship

1. Preservice Music

2. Call to Worship / Invocation

3. Opening Hymn

4. Confession/Absolution

5. Scripture Readings

6. Children's Message

7. Sermon

8. Affirmation of Faith

9. Offering

10. Lord's Prayer/Other Prayers

11. Lord's Supper

12. Benediction

Based on God's Word

____ Psalm 32:5—"I said, 'I will confess my transgressions to the LORD,' and You forgave the iniquity of my sin."

____ Numbers 6:24–26—"The LORD bless you and keep you; the LORD make His face to shine upon you and be gracious to you; the LORD lift up His countenance upon you and give you peace."

____ Jeremiah 17:20—"Hear the Word of the LORD."

____ Psalm 100:2—"Serve the LORD with gladness! Come into His presence with singing!"

____ Matthew 28:19—"In the name of the Father and of the Son and of the Holy Spirit."

____ Matthew 19:14—"Jesus said, 'Let the little children come to Me.'"

____ Luke 11:1—"Lord, teach us to pray."

____ 2 Corinthians 9:7—"Each one must give as he has decided in his heart, not reluctantly or under compulsion, for God loves a cheerful giver."

____ Luke 24:27—"And beginning with Moses and all the Prophets, He interpreted [explained] to them in all the Scriptures."

____ 1 Corinthians 11:26—"As often as you eat this bread and drink the cup, you proclaim the Lord's death until He comes."

____ Isaiah 38:20—"We will play my music on stringed instruments all the days of our lives, at the house of the LORD."

____ Acts 16:31—"Believe in the Lord Jesus, and you will be saved."

Remember

"Be filled with the Spirit, addressing one another in psalms and hymns and spiritual songs, singing and making melody to the Lord with your heart, giving thanks always and for everything to God the Father in the name of our Lord Jesus Christ." (Ephesians 5:18–20)

How does worship today relate to worship in Bible times?

Timeless Worship

Match and discuss Old Testament pictures that relate to pictures of worship in church today.

Timeless Words

Confession	Praise	Teaching	Prayer	Thanks

_____ a. "In the day of my trouble I call upon You." (Psalm 86:7)

_____ b. "Great are the works of the LORD." (Psalm 111:2)

_____ c. "Hide Your face from my sins, and blot out all my iniquities." (Psalm 51:9)

_____ d. "Bless the LORD, O my soul, and forget not all His benefits." (Psalm 103:2)

_____ e. "Your Word is a lamp to my feet and a light to my path." (Psalm 119:105)

Review

Use a thesaurus (printed or online) and find synonyms that mean the same as:

Forever _____

Centered!

Psalm 139

¹O LORD, You have searched me and known me!

²You know when I sit and when I rise up; You discern my thoughts from afar.

³You search out my path and my lying down and are acquainted with all my ways.

⁴Even before a word is on my tongue, behold, O LORD , You know it altogether.

⁵You hem me in, behind and before, and lay Your hand upon me.

⁶Such knowledge is too wonderful for me; it is high; I cannot attain it.

⁷Where can I go from Your Spirit? Or where can I flee from Your presence?

⁸If I ascend to heaven, You are there! If I make my bed in Sheol, You are there!

⁹If I take the wings of the morning and dwell on the uttermost parts of the sea,

¹⁰even there Your hand shall lead me, and Your right hand shall hold me.

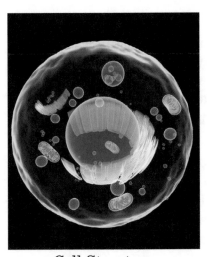

Cell Structure

Solar System

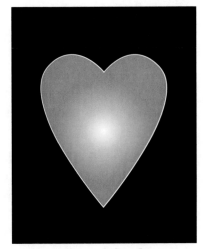

Saved Souls

Remember

"You shall love the Lord your God with all your heart and with all your soul and with all your mind." (Matthew 22:37)

How does the Church Year relate to worship?

The Old Testament Calendar of Festivals

God established the main festivals of the Old Testament year, as recorded in Leviticus 23. The main purpose of each was to **acknowledge God's forgiveness and His blessings to His people.** In turn, the people thanked and praised the Lord. These festivals had different customs and events, but they all involved worship, prayer, special meals, and reminders of historic events that showed God's deliverance and care.

1. **Passover** was celebrated as part of the weeklong **Feast of Unleavened Bread.** It celebrated the night God prepared the people of Israel for His deliverance from their slavery in Egypt.

2. **The Festival of Weeks** was also known as **Pentecost.** It was a thanksgiving day for the recent harvest blessings from God, and it also commemorated God giving the Law to Moses and the people of Israel at Mount Sinai.

3. **The Feast of the Trumpets** is today known as **Rosh Hashanah.** It was a celebration that anticipated the most holy of days soon to come.

4. **The Day of Atonement** (or **Yom Kippur**) was a time of fasting rather than feasting. It was considered the holiest of days, as the people confessed their sins in repentance and the High Priest offered a special sacrifice for the sins of the nation. The High Priest symbolically placed the sins of the people on a goat, who was then sent to the desert to die.

5. **The Feast of Booths** (or **Tabernacles**) was also called **Sukkoth.** It celebrated God's care during Israel's wanderings in the wilderness. In remembrance of this, families built tents or small shelters of branches, eating and even sleeping outdoors in them as their ancestors might have done. This was another type of thanksgiving celebration that lasted for a week.

(Note: Two other festivals were added later: The Festival of Lights [Hanukkah] and the Festival of Esther [Purim], both celebrating times God rescued the people of Israel.)

Review

Propitiation: _____

Atonement: _____

The Christian Church Year

When Jesus came, He fulfilled the promises of the Old Testament, which looked forward to His day. Because of Jesus, we have a New Testament—a new covenant, a new promise in Him. So we celebrate with a new calendar of worship. The first half of the year celebrates **The Life of Christ Jesus.** The second half of the year celebrates **Our Life in Christ Jesus.**

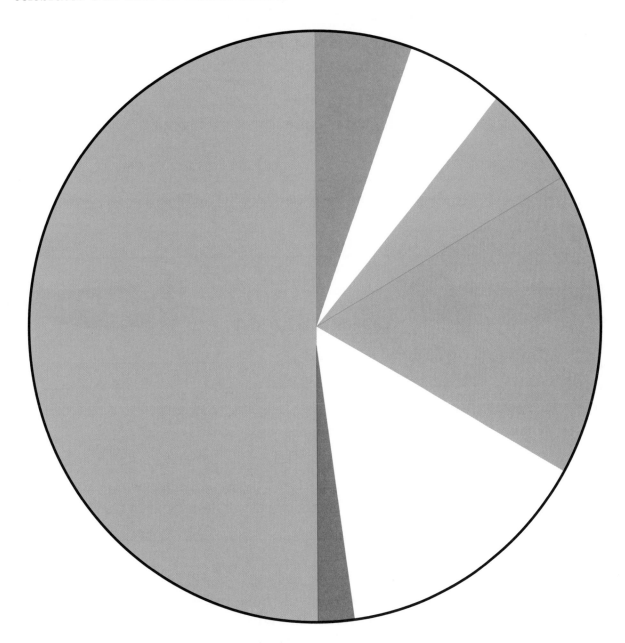

Remember

"I will remember the deeds of the LORD; yes, I will remember Your wonders of old." (Psalm 77:11)

Why do we have worship services for special events?

Significant Life Events

JOHN 2:1–11

- Why would Jesus attend a wedding? _____
  _____

- What difference did Jesus' attendance make at this event?
  _____
  _____

- How did Mary, Jesus' mother, show her trust in God's will at this event?
  _____
  _____

JOHN 11:17–44

- Why would Jesus attend a funeral? _____
  _____
  _____

- What difference did Jesus' attendance make at this event? _____
  _____
  _____

- How did Martha and Mary show their trust in Jesus and in God's will
  at this event? _____
  _____

Jesus' presence and actions at each of these life events shows us that He cares about every aspect of our lives. His will for us is that we trust in Him as our Lord and Savior. Hearing the truth from God's Word at all events in our lives strengthens our faith and assures us of Jesus' power and love.

Review

God's will: _____

Holy matrimony: _____

136

Special Times of Worship

HOLY MATRIMONY (*LSB 275–277*)

- Who began the idea of marriage between a man and a woman?

  _____

  _____

- With what words do a husband or wife make their pledge and promise?

  _____

  _____

  _____

  _____

FUNERAL SERVICE (*LSB 278–281*)

- What life-changing event is remembered and celebrated at the beginning of this service? _____

  _____

  _____

- Why is Jesus' resurrection mentioned so frequently throughout the funeral service? _____

  _____

  _____

Read more about the love and joy we have in Christ in 1 Corinthians 13 and Jeremiah 31:10–14.

Remember

" **A**nd _____ you do, in _____ or _____, do _____ in the name of the Lord _____, giving _____ to _____ the Father through Him." (Colossians 3:17)

What is the background and history of Lutheran hymnody?

God's People Sing

For thousands of years, God's people have worshiped Him by singing. Believers in Old and New Testament times sang psalms, hymns, and other spiritual songs. Often, the psalms were used as hymns by the people in Bible times; a soloist or group of singers would chant the songs while the worshipers listened. Some of these songs were hymns of praise; others were prayers for God's help.

Hymns of the Early Christian Church were written in a style known as plainsong, a form widely used from the fourth century through the eighteenth century. A simple melody in free rhythm was sung with simple or even no accompaniment.

Martin Luther loved music and wanted the congregation to sing in worship services. In 1542, he wrote that music should be "put to proper use and serve its dear Creator and His Christians, that He might be praised and glorified and that we might be bettered and strengthened in the faith through His holy word, driven into the heart with sweet song." (from *What Luther Says: A Practical In-Home Anthology for the Active Christian,* © 1959 CPH, p. 981). Martin Luther wrote thirty-seven hymns. He even wrote a hymn for each part of the catechism to help explain these doctrines. Draw lines to match these hymns of Luther from the *Lutheran Service Book* with the Six Chief Parts of Christian Doctrine.

Hymns Based on the Six Chief Parts

1. The Ten Commandments	a. *LSB* 766
2. The Apostles' Creed	b. *LSB* 607
3. The Lord's Prayer	c. *LSB* 581
4. The Sacrament of Holy Baptism	d. *LSB* 627
5. Confession/Absolution	e. *LSB* 954
6. The Sacrament of the Altar	f. *LSB* 407

Review

Hymn _____

Chant _____

Plainsong _____

Hymns in a New Land

The first Lutheran hymnal, *Etlich Christlich lider*, was published in Wittenberg, Germany in 1524. In 1545, Luther's hymn "Our Father, Who from Heaven Above" was published in Leipzig, Germany in a hymnal called *Geistliche Lieder*. When Christians from Europe moved to the New World, they brought their hymns and hymnals with them. German Lutherans who settled in Pennsylvania, New York, and other eastern states in the 1700s used hymnals that had been published in Germany. These hymnals provided the pattern and the hymns for the first Lutheran hymnal published in America in 1786. It contained 706 hymns, all in German.

Early in 1839, a group of 600 German Lutherans from the region of Saxony arrived in Missouri, followed by 225 more immigrants later that year. They wanted a hymnal with songs that were pure in doctrine for use in public worship. Under the leadership of Pastor C. F. W. Walther, the *Kirchengesangbuch* was published in 1847. At first, this hymnal was the property of Pastor Walther's own congregation in St. Louis. But in 1862, it became the hymnal of The Lutheran Church–Missouri Synod.

Variety and Diversity in Hymns Today

Today, very few Lutherans in America speak or sing hymns in German. But there is a rich heritage in these older hymns, so we continue to sing many of them as English translations. In addition to the hymns Lutherans have sung for centuries, they sing new hymns that reflect our culture of diversity. In the *Lutheran Service Book,* you will find hymns from around the world, from Africa to Japan, and also several in other languages. Look at *LSB* 958 and 959 to compare the same song, presented in English and in Spanish. God hears the voices of all His people, in whatever language they may use to praise His name!

JESUS LOVES ME, THIS I KNOW   (*LOSP,* P. 42)

ENGLISH:
Yes, Jesus loves me,
Yes, Jesus loves me.
Yes, Jesus loves me,
The Bible tells me so.

NAVAJO:
Jesus ayóó áshóní,
Jesus ayóó áshóní,
Jesus ayóó áshóní,
Bizaad yee shithl hal ne.

INDIAN:
Piyar karta, mujh ko,
Piyar karta, mujh ko,
Piyar karta, mujh ko,
Bibúl se m'allum hai.

SPANISH:
Sí, Cristo me ama;
Sí, Cristo me ama;
Sí, Cristo me ama;
La Biblia dice así.

CHINESE:
Ju Yesu nai wo,
Ju Yesu nai wo,
Ju Yesu nai wo,
Shung jing i ko ru wo.

AFRICAN:
Yesu antemwa,
Yesu antemwa,
Yesu antemwa,
Ilandwe lyanjeba.

Remember

"Oh sing to the LORD a new song; sing to the LORD, all the earth!"
(Psalm 96:1)

What is the purpose of word in Lutheran hymnody?

God Prepares a Hymnwriter

The message of God's love and salvation through Jesus is not told in music alone; that message is in the words, or lyrics. This message of the Gospel must be true and Scriptural; that's why the lyrics of hymns are so important. Let's see how God worked through a twentieth century hymn lyric writer to spread God's message.

From the time of his birth on April 28, 1919, God had been preparing Jaroslav Vajda (pronounced YAR-o-slahv VY-dah) to write the words for many beautiful hymns. His parents baptized him, raised him in the faith, and introduced him to his heritage of Slovak language and literature. Jerry Vajda concentrated on his music, playing the violin in the Chicago Youth Symphony by the time he was twelve. Later, he attended Concordia College in Fort Wayne, Indiana and graduated from Concordia Seminary in St. Louis, Missouri in 1944.

He served as a pastor in Pennsylvania, Indiana, and Missouri. Rev. Vajda was the editor of *This Day* magazine from 1963 to 1971 and a book developer for Concordia Publishing House from 1971 to 1986. He also served on the Commission on Worship, evaluating more than two thousand hymn texts. He received many honors, including eight honorary doctorates.

Dr. Vajda published his first hymn, "Now the Silence" (*LSB* 910) in 1969, collaborating with Dr. Carl Schalk, who wrote the music. Over the next forty years, Dr. Vajda was the author of more than two hundred hymn texts and translations. Dr. Schalk and Dr. Vajda collaborated on twenty-six of these. God used many experiences to prepare Jaroslav Vajda for the Lord's work. As the apostle Paul wrote nineteen hundred years earlier, "We are His workmanship, created in Christ Jesus for good works, which God prepared beforehand, that we should walk in them" (Ephesians 2:10).

Jaroslav Vajda said, "Although life has always been a struggle, the church today must speak to the specific concerns of the day. It cannot escape the hungry and the homeless, the oppressed and the captives while at the same time maintaining an optimism that there are divine solutions to the human problems and that Christ is still the only hope the world has."

Now the Joyful Celebration (St. Louis: Morning Star Music Publishers, 1987), p. 9.

COLLABORATE: _____

Psalm 23

1

You, Jesus, are my Shepherd true,

And I your sheep quite helpless;

My ever-loving Guide are you,

Your every thought is selfless;

You feed me, guard me, lead the way

To peace at night and joy by day:

I frolic in your favor.

2

I follow you. The path you choose,

It is the best way for me;

The lamb you love you will not lose,

You walk the way before me;

And though I pass through death's dark vale,

It is my Lord's familiar trail:

I know its glorious ending.

3

Surrounded when I am by foes

Who scorn me or ignore me,

In your strong arms I find repose;

You spread a feast before me!

You welcome me! I find a place

Of honor as your heir of grace,

At home with you forever.

From *Sing of Peace, Sing Gift of Peace,* © 2003 CPH, p318.

Easter Joy!

Walls crack, the trumpet sounds,

the day of jubilee explodes.

The night of feardom gone,

old jails erupt in dancing crowds.

The freedom we parade for

is the freedom Jesus paid for,

So sing a life of gratitude:

Alleluia!

From *Sing of Peace, Sing Gift of Peace,* © 2003 CPH, p272.

Remember

Rearrange the words in the proper order to read today's verse.

Oh LORD song a the to sing new, for things has He marvelous done! His hand arm Him right and have His for salvation holy worked. (Psalm 98:1)

_____

_____

How do we evaluate our hymn and song choices?

Exploring Instruments in Worship

In the box, write the name or draw pictures of instruments you have heard used in a church worship service.

Are you learning to play an instrument? Consider using this talent someday in worship services to offer praise to God. Always remember to keep the main thing the main thing. What is the main thing? _____

(Riddle: Do you know how you can be an instrument?)

Exploring Cultural Influences

From its earliest years, the Christian Church grew strong in Europe, so much of the Church's musical heritage is European (particularly from Italy, Germany, England, and France). Draw a musical note on the map on Europe. When Europeans immigrated to North America and Australia, they brought their European musical heritage with them. Draw a musical note over North America and Australia. Today, the Christian Church is found all over the world, and we are enriched when we share the Christian music of other cultures. Draw musical notes over South America, Asia, and Africa. Add a cross to each continent also as a reminder of the focus of Christian music in all these lands. Today, we continue to add music to this heritage, not just singing 21st century music, but singing the music of 21 centuries of praise to Jesus Christ!

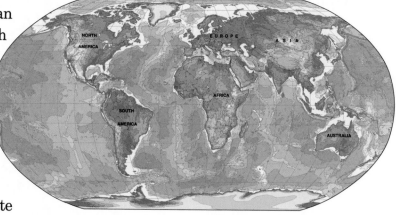

Review

Use a standard dictionary to define these terms.

Culture: _____

Influences: _____

The People Praised the Lord

(King Jehoshaphat—2 Chronicles 20)

1. What was the first thing King Jehoshaphat did when he had a crisis? (vv. 1–3) _____

2. He wasn't alone; who was with him? (v. 13) _____

3. What was the king's plan? (v. 12) _____

4. What words of encouragement came from God's prophet? (v. 15) _____

5. What did the king and the people do when they heard this good news? (vv. 18–19) _____

6. What did the people do the next day when they went out to meet the enemy armies? (v. 21) _____

7. What did God do while the people were singing? (v. 22) _____

8. What did the people do after seeing the defeated army and taking leftover valuables? (v. 26) _____

9. When the people returned home to Jerusalem, what did they do? (v. 28) _____

God continued to bless faithful King Jehoshaphat and his people as they lived in peace (v. 30) and the king did "what was right in the sight of the LORD" (v. 32).

"Worship Wars"

It is sad to say that there have been arguments and battles in churches over matters such as whether we should stand or kneel, whether the pipe organ should be in the front or back of the building, or whether or not to spend money on new carpets. Some people have become bitter enemies over things like this. They have lost sight of what is the main thing in worship. The main thing is that forgiveness and salvation through Christ Jesus be proclaimed in Word and Sacrament in its truth and purity!

Worship Guidelines

(1 Corinthians 14–15)

"Let all things be done for building up" (14:26). "God is not a God of confusion but of peace" (v. 33). "All things should be done decently and in order" (v. 40). "I delivered to you as of *first importance* what I also received: that Christ died for our sins in accordance with the Scriptures" (15:3, emphasis added).

Remember

"'Blessed be the LORD, the God of Israel, from everlasting to everlasting!' Then all the people said, 'Amen!' and praised the LORD." (1 Chronicles 16:36)

How do we praise and thank God wherever we are?

What Do You See?

Discuss your attitude toward these two pictures.

Look at the world cross-eyed!

Jesus loves me, so I _____ . (See 1 John 4:19.)

Jesus forgives me, so I _____ . (See Ephesians 4:32.)

Jesus is kind to me, so I _____ .

Jesus helps me, so I _____ .

Jesus creates good things, so I _____ .

Jesus speaks the truth, so I _____ .

Jesus is dependable, so I _____ .

Jesus is honest, so I _____ .

Jesus is a good friend, so I _____ .

How can I do all this? (See Philippians 4:13.) _____

_____

Review

Attitude: How you look at the world; perspective; viewpoint; point of view; mind-set; outlook; how you observe, understand, and perceive things. Attitudes can be positive or negative. *(If you look for good, you will find it. If you expect problems, they will probably happen.)* Attitudes are affected by viewpoints—things you are partial to or prejudiced against. Your attitude will affect what you see, what you perceive, what you recognize in a situation or circumstance.

Giving Thanks in the Desert—Exodus 14–15

Wherever, Whenever, Whatever

E-TOOLS	USE IN A CHRISTIAN WAY	USE TO PRAISE GOD

Remember

"Give thanks in all circumstances; for this is the will of God in Christ Jesus for you." (1 Thessalonians 5:18)

"Giving thanks always for everything to God the Father in the name of our Lord Jesus Christ." (Ephesians 5:20)

What are the Means of Grace?

Word and Sacrament

John 20:31   Romans 6:4   Corinthians 11:25   Luke 22:19

Review

Grace: Receiving kindness you *do not* deserve.

Mercy: *Not* receiving punishment you *do* deserve.

It's a Gift!

Some of the words in these Bible passages are scrambled. Unscramble them and write them on the line. Then circle the word you wrote and draw an arrow from it to its proper container. If the word is about grace, connect it to the gift box. If the word is not about grace, put it in the trash.

Romans 3:23–24: "For all have _____ and fall short of the

nnisde

_____ of God, and are _____ by His _____ as a

lygro   fitdiejus   cerag

_____ , through the _____ that is in _____ _____."

fitg   medpertion   stCrih   sJsue

Ephesians 2:8–9: "For by _____ you have been _____ through

reacg   devas

_____ . And this is not your own doing; it is the _____ of God, not

itfha   tgif

a result of _____ , so that no one may _____ ."

krswo   tsbao

Romans 6:23: "For the _____ of sin is _____ , but the _____

swega   etadh   eref

_____ of God is _____ _____ in _____ _____ our _____ .

igtf   tenaler   file   tsiCrh   ssueJ   roLd

Remember

"Grace, mercy, and peace will be with us, from God the Father and from Jesus Christ." (2 John 1:3)

Who is to be baptized?

Water and the Word

Directions: Jesus says to baptize "all nations." Read the following Bible verses and tell who this includes.

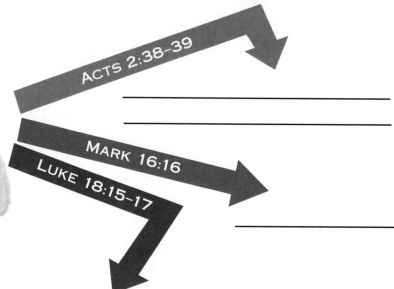

Jesus said, "Go therefore and make disciples of all nations, baptizing them in the name of the Father and of the Son and of the Holy Spirit" (Matthew 28:19).

ACTS 2:38–39 _____

_____

MARK 16:16 ➜
LUKE 18:15–17

_____

TO THINK ABOUT: Reread Mark 16:16. Who is saved? Who is not saved? What does that tell us about Baptism? Mark tells us that whoever believes and is baptized is saved, but he also tells us that whoever does not believe is condemned. Scripture does not say that believers who have not yet been baptized are condemned. Only those who do not believe are condemned. This is seen in today's Bible story. We will see that Paul tells the jailer that he will be saved if he believes in Jesus. Once the jailer believes, he chooses to be baptized, as our Lord commanded. One of the great blessings of God is that He comes to us in several ways to bring us, keep us, and strengthen us in faith. He does this through the Means of Grace, and each means contains the essential Word of God! (If God so graciously offers blessings to us in so many ways, there is no reason any believer would refuse or turn down these gifts, saying, "Thanks, but no thanks!")

The Lord says, "I have redeemed you; I have called you by name, you are Mine" (Isaiah 43:1).

"He is Lord of lords and King of kings, and those with Him are called and chosen and faithful" (Revelation 17:14).

Review

Baptismal Font: Receptacle for water used in Baptism. (What relationship is there between the words *font* and *fountain*? See Psalm 36:9; Zechariah 13:1; *LSB* 435.)

Go Directly to Jail; Do Not Pass Go (Acts 16:16–24)

This document charges

_____ and _____ with being

_____ who are disturbing our

_____. They advocate _____

that are not _____ for us

_____ to accept or _____ .

That is the excuse the magistrates were given for arresting Paul and Silas. The real reason was that Paul and Silas had driven out an evil spirit. The evil spirit had given a slave girl the ability to predict the future, bringing her owners much money. When the girl saw Paul and Silas, the demon inside of her recognized them as "servants of the Most High God" (v. 17). For days, she shouted this out, until Paul became annoyed and commanded the demon to leave the girl. This deprived her owners of easy income, so the owners had them arrested.

"Get Out of Jail Free" Card (Acts 16:25–34)

This card certifies that Paul and Silas were _____ to God and _____ hymns when an _____ set them free. The jailer knelt before Paul and Silas and asked, "What must I do to be _____ ?" They answered him, " _____ in the _____ _____ and you will be saved, you and your _____ ."

Paul and Silas were freed from a man-made jail cell. From what prison was the jailer set free? _____ The jailer was so joyful! With whom did he share the good news? _____ What risk did he take? _____

Remember

"As many of you as were baptized into Christ have put on Christ.
. . . You are all one in Christ Jesus." (Galatians 3:27–28)

What are the blessings of Baptism?

What Does Luther Say?

In the Small Catechism, Martin Luther explains that God comes to us in Baptism and gives us gifts of forgiveness and salvation. Baptism is not something we do; it is something we receive as God's gift.

What benefits does Baptism give?

It works forgiveness of sins, rescues from death and the devil, and gives eternal salvation to all who believe this, as the words and promises of God declare.

How can water do such great things?

Certainly not just water, but the word of God in and with the water does these things, along with the faith which trusts this word of God in the water. For without God's word the water is plain water and no Baptism. But with the word of God it is a Baptism, that is, a life-giving water, rich in grace, and a washing of the new birth in the Holy Spirit.

Unexpected Events!

Finish each sentence by filling in the unexpected events of Pentecost (Acts 2):

1. Galileans who usually spoke only one language could _____

_____ .

2. Earlier, Peter denied Jesus, but now _____

_____ .

3. Jesus was crucified and buried, but now _____ .

4. The church grew from 120 believers to _____ .

5. People are baptized and receive _____

_____ .

Review

Pentecost (Old Testament times): _____

_____

Pentecost (New Testament times): _____

_____

Uncommon Gifts!

A.

B.

C.

D.

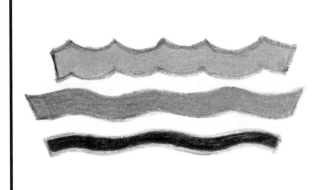

Remember

"He saved us . . . by the washing of regeneration and renewal of the Holy Spirit, whom He poured out on us richly through Jesus Christ our Savior, so that being justified by His grace we might become heirs according to the hope of eternal life. The saying is trustworthy." (Titus 3:5–8)

What does my Baptism long ago mean for me today?

Plenty of Water

Consider the average number of times per day you do the following activities. Multiply that number by 365 days per year and an average life span of 75 years. Approximately how many times in your life will you

wash your hands? _____

brush your teeth? _____

have a drink of water? _____

take a shower? _____

wash the dishes? _____

get baptized? _____

receive the blessings of Baptism? _____

Drowning in Water

Baptism is not just a past event; it is part of who we are. Its blessings continue each day, for we are forgiven and baptized people of God.

> IN THE SMALL CATECHISM, BAPTISM, FOURTH PART, MARTIN LUTHER SAYS:
> *What does such baptizing with water indicate?*
>
> It indicates that the Old Adam in us should by daily contrition and repentance be drowned and die with all sins and evil desires, and that a new man should daily emerge and arise to live before God in righteousness and purity forever.

Martin Luther's words are based on Scripture: 2 Corinthians 5:17 says, "If anyone is in Christ, he is a new creation," and Ephesians 4:24 says, "Put on the new self, created after the likeness of God in true righteousness and holiness." God's power enables us to live as His baptized people and as the children of God.

Review

Regeneration: Spiritual rebirth, becoming **new again**.

Renewal: To **begin again**, restored to a condition that had been lost or damaged.

Powerful Water

Genesis 7:17–24

What was drowned in the flood waters?

_____

_____

_____

What did the floodwaters do for Noah and

his family? _____

_____

_____

What changes did the flood waters make?

_____

_____

_____

1 Peter 3:18–22

What is drowned in the waters of Baptism?

_____

_____

_____

What do the waters of Baptism do for the

person? _____

_____

_____

What changes occur in the life of a person

who is baptized? _____

_____

_____

Remember

"Do you not know that all of us who have been baptized into Christ Jesus were baptized into His death? We were buried therefore with Him by baptism into death, in order that, just as Christ was raised from the dead by the glory of the Father, we too might walk in newness of life." (Romans 6:3–4)

What is happening during the Lord's Supper?

Going to the Lord's Table

In some ways, the Lord's Supper is a lot like a family birthday meal or the celebration many families enjoy at Thanksgiving or Christmas. We get out the best dishes and a real linen tablecloth. We may use cloth napkins instead of paper ones. Everyone is on his or her best behavior. Some families light candles. We want everyone we love to be there with us. In a similar way, many churches use their very best dishes—or altarware—for the Lord's Supper. The chalice may be silver and ornately decorated. The altar cloths (paraments) are starched, ironed, and arranged just so. The acolyte may light candles that are lit only for Communion services. The pastor may wear a sleeveless robe (a *chasuble*), something he wears only at Communion, over his other robes. We invite everyone in our faith family, everyone close to us in faith and love, to be together to share Jesus' forgiveness and peace with us. The Lord's Supper is similar to some family celebrations, but it differs from them too. What differences can you name?

It's a Mystery!

B B R O E D A Y D

B W L I O N O E D

> in, with, under <

_____

_____

It's a Treasure!

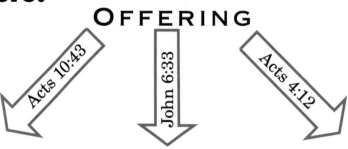

O F F E R I N G

Acts 10:43   John 6:33   Acts 4:12

_____   _____   _____

Review

Is the Lord's Supper a sacrament? Check off each statement that applies.

☐ A sacred act instituted by God.

☐ God has joined His Word of promise to a visible element.

☐ God offers the forgiveness of sins earned by Christ.

What Is This Mystery?

KEY QUESTIONS	SCRIPTURE'S ANSWERS	HYMN RESPONSE
WHAT IS THIS BREAD?	1 Corinthians 11:23–24	*LSB* 629:1
WHAT IS THIS WINE?	1 Corinthians 11:25	*LSB* 629:2
SO WHO AM I?	1 Corinthians 11:26	*LSB* 629:3
YET IS GOD HERE?	Luke 22:19–20	*LSB* 629:4
IS THIS FOR ME?	Luke 22:14–17	*LSB* 629:5

Remember

"For as often as you eat this bread and drink the cup, you proclaim the Lord's death until He comes." (1 Corinthians 11:26)

We are baptized once; why does the Lord's Supper happen often?

The Family Gathers

The Sacraments relate to some things that happen in a family. You are born or adopted into a family only once, but you eat supper with the family often. In the family of God, our rebirth or adoption into His family happens once, when we are baptized, but we gather together often for the Lord's Supper. We know God loves the whole world, but He also wants us to know that He cares about each of us individually. God comes to us in the Sacraments, touching our lives and assuring us personally and directly that He loves and forgives each one of us.

In Days of Old, when Saints Were Bold

Across

2. What all the people felt as they saw what Jesus was doing through His Church.
5. Belongings, the things one owns.
7. Another word for a "teaching."
8. Day by day, the Lord _____ new believers to His Church.
9. The believers held all their possessions in _____ .

Down

1. The early Christians came together here to worship.
2. Men trained by Jesus and sent by Him to lead the Early Church.
3. Another name for "the breaking of bread."
4. The hearts of the believers were glad and _____.
6. Another word for *miracle*.

Review

Communicant: Someone who is eligible to receive Holy Communion. As I think about the Lord's Supper, the main reasons I want to participate is _____

_____

Challenges Today

Boldly Speaking Out

When brought before a council of leaders and ordered to not speak about Jesus, Peter boldly said:

"We cannot but speak of what we have seen and heard" (Acts 4:20).

"There is salvation in no one else, for there is no other name under heaven given among men by which we must be saved" (Acts 4:12).

Observed by Others

As Christianity spread, even enemies could see the powerful influence of Christ and His Church:

Gamaliel to a group of Pharisees: **"If this plan or this undertaking is of man, it will fail; but if it is of God, you will not be able to overthrow them. You might even be found opposing God!" (Acts 5:38–39).**

Angry mob to city leaders: **"These men *who have turned the world upside down* have come here also" (Acts 17:6).**

Remember

"Oh, taste and see that the LORD is good!" (Psalm 34:8)

Who is worthy to receive the Lord's Supper?

How God Looks at Greatness

1 Read Matthew 18:1–4. The disciples were interested in who was the greatest. Jesus answered by saying that greatness is in the sincere and simple faith of _____ . Turn to the next chapter (19:13–15). Did the disciples learn the lesson Jesus taught? _____ How can you tell? _____

2 The same problem came up again: pride and self-centeredness. Turn to the next chapter and read 20:17–28. Jesus probably wondered if His disciples would ever learn! (He probably wonders that about us too!) Jesus told His disciples that whoever wanted to be great must become a _____ , willingly helping others. Turn to the next chapter (21:1–9) and read. What great event was about to happen? _____

3 Now it was time for the Passover celebration. Jesus gave His disciples the new covenant of the Lord's Supper. Surely, they would finally understand—or maybe not. Read Luke 22:24–26. The disciples needed lots of forgiveness from Jesus. Who else needs lots of forgiveness? _____ Jesus patiently demonstrated His greatness through His _____ , as He washed the disciples' feet. Read John 13:12–17. What did Jesus want His disciples (and you and me) to do? _____ (Read verses 34–35.)

4 That very next day, Good Friday, Jesus demonstrated the greatest love of all as He died on the cross to take the punishment for our sins. "Greater love has no one than this, that someone lay down his life for his friends" (John 15:13).

Review

A. Greatness in the world: _____

B. Greatness in God's kingdom: _____

Back to the Original Question

So, who is worthy to receive the Lord's Supper?

- If you think you are great, you are wrong.

- If you think you can do something to be worthy, you are wrong.

- If you don't recognize that you need forgiveness, you are wrong.

- If you don't believe Jesus offers forgiveness in the Sacrament, you are wrong.

> When do we receive the Sacrament worthily?
> We receive it worthily when we have faith in Christ and His words, "Given and shed for you for the forgiveness of sins."
>
> (From *Luther's Small Catechism with Explanation*, Question 301)

When God looks at our hearts, this is what He wants to see: hearts made worthy through the redemption and righteousness Jesus gives us. He wants to see that in humility,

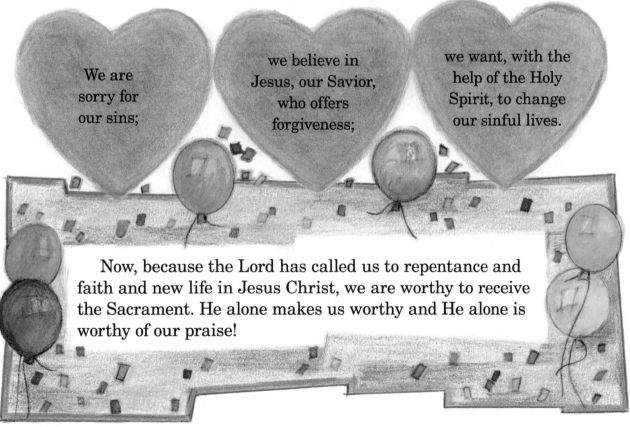

We are sorry for our sins;

we believe in Jesus, our Savior, who offers forgiveness;

we want, with the help of the Holy Spirit, to change our sinful lives.

Now, because the Lord has called us to repentance and faith and new life in Jesus Christ, we are worthy to receive the Sacrament. He alone makes us worthy and He alone is worthy of our praise!

Remember

"The Son of Man came not to be served but to serve, and to give His life as a ransom for many." (Matthew 20:28)

How does the Passover relate to the Lord's Supper?

A Preview

Directions: Read Exodus 12:1–13, 23–35. Cross off the wrong answer inside each parentheses. Watch out for one trick answer.

After sending (nine fourteen) plagues on Egypt, God told Moses there would be one more disaster. After this last plague, Pharaoh would not only let the people go, but he would also urge them to (stay leave). The people of Israel were to make special (clothing preparations). Each family was to choose their best lamb—one with no (defects name)—for a special meal. Along with the roast (beef lamb), the people ate (bitter sweet) herbs to remind them of the (bitterness happiness) of slavery. They ate unleavened bread, because they would be leaving in a (boat hurry); there was no time to let the yeast in the bread rise, so they ate flat, hard bread. As a special sign, they were to put some of the lamb's (wool blood) on the tops and sides of the (windows doorposts) of their houses. That night at (midnight 3 a.m.), the Lord passed over the homes with the special sign. In all the other homes in Egypt, the (youngest firstborn) (son daughter) of the family died. There was great sadness in the homes of the people who had (believed rejected) the Word of the Lord. The people begged the Israelites to leave, for they were afraid that everyone in Egypt would soon (die cry). The Egyptians (took offered) silver, gold, and other valuables. The Israelites were finally free, not because of their own doing, but because of the mighty power of (Moses, God). More than a million people were now on their way to the (land city) God had promised to Abraham, Isaac, and (Jacob Esau). Each year, the people of Israel were to celebrate the Passover to remember again the day God delivered them from (slavery bondage).

A Promise

The night before Jesus died on the cross, He and His disciples celebrated the Passover meal. Then Jesus announced a new change, a new covenant, and a new agreement between God and humankind by celebrating a new meal: the Lord's Supper. Knowing that He Himself was the Lamb of God that would be sacrificed, Jesus took bread and wine from the Passover meal, saying this is His body and blood, given for the forgiveness of our sins. He said we are to do this often in remembrance of Him.

Review

Testament: A declaration; a covenant.

Covenant: A promise or pledge; a formal agreement.

Shadows and Son Light

The Passover "foreshadowed," or gave a glimpse of, what was to come. Write a comparative statement showing how Jesus has fulfilled or completed each preview, bringing to light God's plan of salvation for us.

THE OLD COVENANT (TESTAMENT)	THE NEW COVENANT (TESTAMENT)
a. For many years, the people of Israel were slaves in Egypt.	
b. God freely offered deliverance to His people.	
c. A lamb was sacrificed for the Passover.	
d. Those who believed and trusted God's Word were rescued.	
e. The people of Israel were saved from the power of Pharaoh.	
f. The people rejoiced in the gift of freedom.	
g. The people continued to celebrate the Passover, remembering God's grace.	

Remember

"Jesus answered them, 'Truly, truly, I say to you, everyone who commits sin is a slave to sin. . . . If the Son sets you free, you will be free indeed.' " (John 8:34, 36)

What is the role of the "Christian Questions with Their Answers"?

Examinations! Why?

Though tests are often called exams, an examination is usually more thorough and complete. An examination goes beyond knowing the right and wrong answers. It analyzes the situation, identifies problems, and suggests a course of action. An examination checks to see if you can function and if you can apply what you know. Discuss the significance of these examinations.

A Heart Examination

In Bible times, Corinth was the largest Greek city. It was a center for business and trade.

The Church the apostle Paul started there began strong (1 Corinthians 1:1–9), but then problems started.

1. What was Paul's analysis of the situation? (1 Corinthians 11:17–18)

_____

_____

2. Eating a meal with friends can be a good thing. What was wrong with it in this situation? (1 Corinthians 11:20–21) _____

_____

3. What did Paul recommend? (1 Corinthians 11:28; see also 10:31) _____

_____

_____

Review

Worthy: *Deserving, honorable, upright, of value.*

Self-Examination

Martin Luther included a list of questions and answers in the Small Catechism so that we would have a tool to use to examine our lives as Christians. This self-examination helps us remember why we need Jesus. Look at this list, called "Christian Questions with Their Answers," either in the Appendix of this book or in *LSB* (pp. 329–30). Use the questions (such as Q 1) and answers to fill in the blanks.

I am a _____ because I have disobeyed the _____. I am
(Q 1)   (Q 2)

_____ for my sins. Because I am a sinner, I deserve only _____
(Q 3)   (Q 4)

from God. I _____ to be saved; in fact, I know I will be saved, because I
(Q 5)

_____ in Jesus. He _____ His blood for me on the cross so that
(Q 6)   (Q 9)

I now have _____. I know this is true from Jesus' words in the _____,
(Q 9)   (Q 11)

where He says He gives His body and blood for me. When Jesus instituted the Sacrament

of the Lord's Supper, He said we receive the _____ of sins and that we
(Q 12)

are to do this often in _____ of Him. I believe the words of Jesus when He
(Q 16)

says that His _____ body and blood are in the Sacrament. When we take
(Q 13–14)

the Lord's Supper, we remember and _____ to other people that we believe
(Q 15)

we are saved by Jesus. Only through Jesus do we have the _____ and
(Q 16)

_____ of salvation. Jesus died and made full payment for our sins
(Q 16)

because of His _____ love for us. We are encouraged to go to the Sacrament
(Q 17)

often because of the _____ and the _____ of Christ the Lord.
(Q 19)   (Q 19)

Remember

[Jesus said,] "Do this in remembrance of Me." (Luke 22:19)

What is confirmation?

Making a Commitment

Read Psalm 119:105–112. What do these verses say about the power of God's Word in our lives?

Verse 105 _____

Verse 107 _____

Verse 111 _____

The word *commitment* means "an agreement or pledge to do something in the future." What has the psalmist committed to do according to these verses?

Verse 106 _____

Verse 109 _____

Verse 110 _____

Verse 112 _____

Samuel's Lifelong Commitment

Dedicated
to God

| Born | Four years | Twelve years | Young man | Old man |

"Be faithful _____ " (Revelation 2:10).

You Are Just Beginning!

SHELLY JEAN
BAPTIZED
6/12/01

BAPTIZED 6/12/01
CONFIRMED 5/20/14
Revelation 2:10

Review

Vow: A solemn promise, made before God and witnesses; to make a personal commitment regarding actions in the future.

What Is Confirmation?

Connection to your Baptism: reaffirming what you believe.

Commitment to the future: pledging lifelong faithfulness.

Factors to Consider

Chief Parts (Six) of Christian Doctrine: studied in preparation.

Confession of faith: publicly stating what you believe.

Courage: remember that it's not about you, it's about God.

Christian community: the Church surrounds and supports you.

Customs: may vary from place to place.

Continue: in worship, serving others, living for Jesus, and glorifying God.

Remember

Rewrite the words scrambled in italics: "Continue in what you have learned and have *fmlyir* _____ believed, knowing from whom you learned it and how from childhood you have been acquainted with the *redsac* _____ writings, which are able to make you *sewi* _____ for salvation through *aifht* _____ in Christ Jesus." (2 Timothy 3:14–15)

What are liturgical arts?

Symbols of the Twelve Disciples

PETER

PHILIP

IXΘYC

JAMES

JOHN

ANDREW

THOMAS

?
?
?
?

Review

Liturgical Arts: Various skills, methods, and media used in the development of religious materials or the construction of a church sanctuary in order to proclaim a message of God's grace, particularly through Christ Jesus, and to give glory to God in all things.

MATTHEW

THADDAEUS

JAMES THE LESS

SIMON THE ZEALOT

BARTHOLOMEW

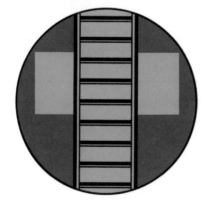

JUDAS ISCARIOT

Remember

"**W**hatever you do, in word or deed, do everything in the name of the Lord Jesus." (Colossians 3:17)

Who is my neighbor?

First Table of the Law

Love God above all.

Honor God's holy name.

Respect and hear God's Word.

Second Table of the Law

My neighbor is _____

_____

    We live in a global society. We are connected to people around the world by communication (such as _____), by transportation (such as _____), and by commerce (check where your shirt and shoes were made). We also have a special connection to people all over the world who have _____

_____. (See Luke 24:45–48.)

Review

Synonyms of Law: commandment, statute, rule, command, instruction, decree, ordinance, requirement, regulation, mandate, precept, order, direction, summons, obligation.

David's Life

David's life was filled with many antonyms (opposites). He was a son, father; shepherd, soldier; friend, fugitive; musician to the king, and crowned king. He was courageous, a coward; faithful, a sinner; joyful, saddened; foolish, and wise. Above all, he was called to repentance and forgiveness by God! As you look at just one of David's stories, cross off each underlined word and write its antonym.

2 Samuel 9: The <u>last</u> _____ king of Israel was Saul. King Saul <u>loved</u>

_____ David, but his son Jonathan was David's <u>enemy</u> _____. Even

though Saul tried to <u>rescue</u> _____ David, David promised to <u>destroy</u>

_____ the members of the royal family. Years later, when David became

the <u>queen</u> _____, he sent for Jonathan's son Mephibosheth, who was <u>rich</u>

_____ and crippled in both <u>hands</u> _____. Mephibosheth feared the king

would <u>help</u> _____ him because of his grandfather Saul. Instead, King David

showed <u>cruelty</u> _____ because of Mephibosheth's father, Jonathan.

My Life

Jesus fulfilled the Law in our place, He forgives us when we break God's Law, and He empowers us through the Means of Grace to live according to God's will in the Law. What does Scripture say is the true fulfillment of the Law? See Romans 13:10. _____

Use a red marker or crayon to change each Table of the Law to a heart. Read the passages to find ways to fulfill the Law with loving kindness.

Proverbs 31:9

Philippians 2:4

Romans 13:7

Hebrews 13:16

Ephesians 4:32

Remember

[Jesus said,] "You shall love the Lord your God with all your heart and with all your soul and with all your mind. This is the great and first commandment. And a second is like it: You shall love your neighbor as yourself." (Matthew 22:37–39)

What leaders should I obey?

Who Is In Charge Here?

1. Identify people in various roles of authority. _____

_____

_____

2. Why is it often difficult to obey those in authority? _____

_____

_____

3. Identify characteristics of a good leader. _____

_____

4. Where does the authority of a leader come from? _____

_____

_____

5. What do you personally need to do to be a good leader? _____

_____

_____

_____

6. Who is the ultimate authority? _____

_____

Review

Authority: Having power to make decisions and to establish or enforce commands and rules.

Consecrate: To set someone or something apart for a special, holy purpose.

Obedient to a Leader and as a Leader

God looked at the heart of David. It was not a perfect heart, but it was a repentant heart—a heart forgiven by God. We can join David as he spoke of this forgiveness and salvation in Psalm 24:5; 25:6–7; 32:1–5; 38:22; 103:11–12.

P. S. A Prelude and a Postlude

A *prelude* is something that "comes before." A prelude to David's obedience was the disobedience and unrepentance of King Saul, who disobeyed God's command, lied about it, and blamed it on others (1 Samuel 15:20–21). Read about the consequence of Saul's sins in 1 Samuel 15:26–28. A *postlude* is something that "comes after." Sometime after King David's reign, Rehoboam, David's grandson, became king. He did not follow the ways of his grandfather and was not obedient to God's ways and will. Read about his foolishness in 1 Kings 12:6–11. The consequence was that many people turned away from him, split the kingdom, and chose a new king for themselves. After this, there was a northern kingdom of Israel and a southern kingdom of Judah.

Remember

"Remind them to be submissive to rulers and authorities, to be obedient, to be ready for every good work, to speak evil of no one, to avoid quarreling, to be gentle, and to show perfect courtesy toward all people." (Titus 3:1–2)

What does it mean to respect life?

The Fifth Commandment: You shall not murder.

What does this mean? We should fear and love God so that we do not hurt or harm our neighbor in his body, but help and support him in every physical need.

A Big Issue

At first glance, you might think that this commandment is for criminals, but it is a much bigger issue than that. The Fifth Commandment is not just about MURDER. It is also about LIFE! God gives life and He expects us to value life. Because of this, taking away life in abortion, euthanasia, and suicide are also sins against God's commandment. People who take away life in any of these ways are placing their own will above the will of God, which is also breaking the First Commandment; they are, in effect, taking on God's role by deciding who lives and for how long.

Setting the Standard

How do you decide if something is right or wrong? Circle the right answer.

> a. By taking a vote to make it legal.

> b. By observing that "everybody does it."

> c. By learning if it is according to God's will.

The bottom line is: __ e __ __ e __ __   __i __ e.

Review

Abortion: Taking the life of an unborn person.

Euthanasia: Ending the life of someone too infirm or helpless to care for himself or herself.

Suicide: Taking one's own life.

"The God who made the world and everything in it, . . . He Himself gives to all mankind life and breath and everything." (Acts 17:24–25)

David Follows the Lord

Once again, we will take a look at the life of David. Twice, he had the opportunity to murder someone who was trying to murder him. With a partner, study these parallel accounts, comparing the two incidents and locating the verses that correspond with the sentences.

	1 SAMUEL	
	CHAPTER 24	CHAPTER 26
1. King Saul and his army chased after David, trying to kill him.		
2. David had a chance to get rid of his enemy.		
3. David's friends encouraged him to kill Saul.		
4. David refused to harm the Lord's anointed king.		
5. David took tokens or signs of his mercy.		
6. David called Saul's attention to the evidence.		
7. King Saul was sorry about his jealous, angry actions.		
8. David and Saul went their separate ways.		

The Lord Guides Us

Jesus came to fulfill the Law perfectly in our place and to take our punishment for our sins against the Law. Now God's Law serves as a guide for the sanctified lives we live for Christ, as empowered by the Holy Spirit. In the Sermon on the Mount, in Matthew 5, Jesus tells us to not just look at God's Law as something we have to do and do exactly according to the letter of the law, but He also tells us that as Christians we should go *beyond* the Law, taking *extra* steps of kindness and mercy to others. Summarize what Jesus says to us in these statements.

1. Matthew 5:21–22: Jesus said, "You have heard, . . . 'You shall not murder,' . . . but I say to you": _____

2. Matthew 5:33–37: Jesus said, "You have heard, . . . 'You shall not swear falsely,' . . . but I say to you": _____

3. Matthew 5:38–42: Jesus said, "You have heard, . . . 'An eye for an eye,' . . . but I say to you": _____

4. Matthew 5:43–48: Jesus said, "You have heard, . . . 'You shall love your neighbor and hate your enemy,' . . . but I say to you": _____

Remember

[Jesus said,] "I came that they may have LIFE and have it ABUNDANTLY." (John 10:10b)

What is a chaste and decent life?

The Sixth Commandment and Sex

SEX IS NOT A SHOCKING WORD!

Your sex is your gender: either male or female.
Male or female is how God created you.

What is shocking is how sex is misused!

The Sixth Commandment and Sin

People sin by what they

Think	Say	Do

King David and the Sixth Commandment

2 Samuel 11–12   Psalm 32

used someone else to kill—but it's still murder

evil plan to put someone in harm's way

attempted cover-up with lies and deception

an affair with another man's wife

sinful thoughts

Review

Chaste: morally and sexually clean and pure.

Decent: meeting accepted standards of moral behavior.

Morality: good character or behavior that follows a value system of right and wrong.

Modest: humble in appearance.

Pure: innocent, without guilt, free from impurities.

Who(se) Are You?

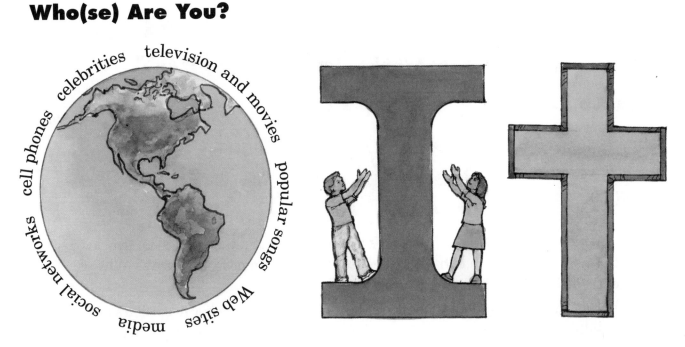

The Bottom Line(s)

Use God's gifts and blessings to:

Respect _ o u _ _ e _ _ and o _ _ e _ _.

G _ o _ i _ _ God in a _ _ _ _ i _ _ _.

Remember

"The peace of God, which surpasses all understanding, will guard your hearts and your minds in Christ Jesus." (Philippians 4:7)

"Whatever is ☐☐☐, whatever is ☐☐☐☐☐☐☐, whatever is ☐☐☐☐, whatever is ☐☐☐☐, whatever is ☐☐☐☐☐, whatever is ☐☐☐☐☐☐☐☐☐, if there is any ☐☐☐☐☐☐☐, if there is anything ☐☐☐☐☐ of praise, think about these things." (Philippians 4:8)

Is stealing a sin we sometimes don't even recognize?

"I'm No Fool!"

Discuss: How are each of these actually examples of stealing—taking what isn't yours?

1. Romondo has a new skill—shoplifting. He's gotten so good at it that he's taken five new DVDs from the store in the past month without getting caught. "I'm no fool," he says. "Why pay if you can get them for nothing?"

2. Mrs. Wright hires Shelly to weed her flower bed, promising to pay her five dollars an hour. There really aren't that many weeds, and Shelly still needs ten dollars to get the new sweater she wants. So she takes her time—lots of time—as she works. "I'm no fool," she thinks. "Mrs. Wright has plenty of money, and I really want that sweater!"

3. Mrs. Wright hires Sandra to weed her flower bed, promising to pay her five dollars an hour. Sandra works really hard for two hours. When Sandra is done, Mrs. Wright comes to the door and gives her an envelope. When Sandra gets home and opens the envelope, it contains only eight dollars. "I'm no fool," Mrs. Wright says to herself. "Kids her age don't work as hard as they should."

4. One day after school, Scott's dad takes him along to the gym. Dad gives Scott money to get two bottles of water from a vending machine. Scott puts the money in, a bottle falls out, and all the money drops back into the change return too! Scott puts it back into the slot, gets a second bottle of water, and all the money falls back out into the change return slot again! Scott pockets the money and takes the two bottles of water. "I'm no fool," he thinks. "It's mine now."

5. TJ and Travis are playing in the snow. The temperature is just right for making snowballs. TJ puts two rocks inside a big snowball and heaves it at a passing car—and breaks one of the side windows! The boys take off running in the opposite direction. "I'm no fool," thinks TJ. "If they can't catch me, I won't have to pay for the damages!"

6. Whenever Katia goes to a restaurant, she orders water with her food, but she fills her cup with a soft drink. "I'm no fool," she says. "These places make plenty of profit on their food."

7. Jake walks across the playground and sees his brother's jacket lying in the grass. Kevin is nowhere in sight. "That knot head!" Jake thinks. "He's always getting into trouble for losing his things. I could take it home, but I'm no fool. That's his problem, not mine."

Review

> **Materialism:** 1. An intense focus on physical things, comforts, or possessions.
>
> 2. A false trust that looks to possessions to make one happy or secure.

Nabal, the Fool

Listen as your teacher tells the narrative based on 1 Samuel 25:1–39. Then talk together about these questions:

• The name *Nabal* means "Fool." In what ways was Nabal foolish?

• In what ways was David foolish?

• How did Abigail show godly wisdom?

God's Wisdom

Maybe you've never thought before today about the many ways we can break the Seventh Commandment. Burglars and bank robbers sin against God's command, but so do shoplifters, time wasters, and computer game copiers. By sinning against the Seventh Commandment, we earn God's punishment. Stealing in any of the ways we've talked about carries the death penalty: the eternal death penalty! That's really bad news. But thank God, we also know the good news: Jesus died for all our sins—every one of them, including sins of stealing. When we confess our sins, God forgives. With His forgiveness, He also gives us the courage and wisdom it takes to show we're sorry by making amends, even if that is scary! Talk about these two questions with your class:

• What's the worst news you've learned in this lesson?

• What's the best news you've learned in this lesson?

Remember

"Let each of you look not only to his own interests, but also to the interests of others. Have this mind among yourselves, which is yours in Christ Jesus." (Philippians 2:4–5)

Do I honor God with my words?

Sticks and Stones

Have you heard this old rhyme? "Sticks and stones may break my bones, but words will never hurt me." This rhyme is untrue! Words can often be even more hurtful than physical harm. In the Fifth and Seventh Commandments God wants us to protect other people from bodily harm and to protect their property. In the Eighth Commandment, our Lord expects us to defend the reputations of other people. In the following section, put an X in three boxes next to those situations you think would hurt someone the most.

☐ 1. A classmate tells your teacher you copied his homework, even though you didn't.

☐ 2. A friend talks two other friends into believing you stole money from her desk.

☐ 3. A sixth grader tells your friends that the police are going to arrest your uncle.

☐ 4. You tell your best friend a secret. Now your friend is telling it to everybody.

☐ 5. All the kids in your class are looking at you and laughing. You don't know why until you see your picture hanging in the restroom with an unflattering caption printed next to it.

☐ 6. Every time your neighbor sees you, he calls you "little wart." Your friends think it's hilarious, but you are embarrassed.

☐ 7. Two of your teammates make up lies about you in the car pool. Your best friend says nothing to defend you! Now the driver won't let her twins invite you to their birthday party.

Why do you think you and so many other people say bad things about other people?

_____

_____

_____

No Broken Bones

The Eighth Commandment: You shall not give false testimony against your neighbor. *What does this mean?* We should fear and love God so that we do not tell lies about our neighbor, betray him, slander him, or hurt his reputation, but defend him, speak well of him, and explain everything in the kindest way.

Review

> **Betray:** To tell someone's secrets; to act disloyally.
>
> **Slander:** To spread malicious or false rumors.
>
> **Reputation:** The respect and value in which someone's character is regarded.
>
> **Gossip:** Telling someone's personal or private matters.

It Takes Courage! *(1 Samuel 20)*

If you defend someone:

1. Your friends might laugh at you and call you names.

2. They may avoid you, breaking off friendships.

3. They may turn on you and hurt you.

4. Your best friend _____ _____.

The Kindest Way

Question A: What if the negative things spoken about someone are true?

_____

_____

_____

Question B: Who speaks up for you? (See Romans 8:31–34, 37–39.) _____

_____

Question C: As a Christian child of God, how are you to use words? (See Proverbs 31:8–9; Psalm 51:15.) _____

_____

Question D: As a child of God, led by the Spirit, what will be our attitude? (See the parable in Luke 7:31–32. Also read 1 Corinthians 13:6–7.) Define *sympathy* and *empathy*.

_____

_____

_____

Remember

"Encourage one another and build one another up."

(1 Thessalonians 5:11)

Why are coveting thoughts sinful?

A Matter of Attitude

Coveting leads to **greed.** Mr. Keller coveted money. He never had enough, even when he had a million dollars. He was never satisfied, even when he had a billion dollars. When asked how much money he wanted, he answered, "More."

Coveting leads to **envy.** Marcia said, "I hate Emma. She won the spelling bee and the geography bee. She plays the piano and the flute (but not at the same time). Now she got first place in track. Who wants a stupid blue ribbon anyway?" "I think you do," said her sister Sarah. "You want what Emma has and you are envious!"

Coveting leads to **rivalry.** Reggie was having a temper tantrum as he shouted, "Mom, you just have to take me to the mall! This is important. I need to get two new baseball hats because Jeremy came to school today wearing a new one. I can't let him outdo me."

Coveting leads to **scheming.** Quanisha had always wanted a sweater like Tina's. Now Tina had lost the sweater, and both girls looked everywhere for it. Finally, Quanisha spotted the sweater under the steps. She decided not to say a word about it; once Tina went home, Quanisha could keep the sweater. After all, "finders, keepers; losers, weepers."

Review

Check a dictionary. Write the definitions.

Rivalry: _____

Covet: _____

Envy: _____

Greed: _____

Coveting leads to deceit.

Bobby was just four years old. He couldn't wait to show his ten-year-old cousin Randall the two dollar bills he got for his birthday. Randall pretended to be unimpressed, saying, "Just two of them? How about trading them for these six quarters. You know that six is a lot more than two."

Coveting leads to pretense.

Sharla said, "Today is my lucky day. I gave the clerk at the toy store ten dollars. She thought I gave her twenty dollars, so I got all this extra money back. It's her fault: she should have been more careful." Sharla pretended to be innocent, as if she had a right to the money, but she knew the money belonged to someone else.

Christ leads to change.

Christ leads to change. This would be a hopeless picture without Jesus. Only He can make a difference as He calls us through the Means of Grace to repentance, faith, and forgiveness. Jesus takes away the sin from our hearts and the Holy Spirit fills them with the love, peace, and joy that only He can bring. What a change!

Christ leads to gratitude.

Christ leads to gratitude. What is the opposite of coveting the things of this world? Gratitude for the many blessings of God! When we recognize, appreciate, and enjoy God's gifts to us, our hearts are filled!

Remember

"Keep your life free from love of money,* and be content with what you have, for [God] has said, 'I will never leave you nor forsake you.' "

(Hebrews 13:5)

*What other things besides money might people covetously love?

How can we find contentment?

More Coveting

From the Ninth Commandment, we learned that coveting is wanting what belongs to someone else and not being content with what we have. We learned that coveting can lead to greed, envy, jealousy, rivalry, scheming, deceit, and pretense. Today, we will see that the Tenth Commandment is also about coveting—except it is about coveting *relationships*. This kind of coveting leads to some of the same problems and same sins. In light of the forgiveness of sins and the new life we have in Christ, what advice would you give these people, who covet other relationships with family and friends?

- "My friend Jessica's parents let her go to the mall and to the movies whenever she wants. My parents never let me do anything, and I have to call them all the time if I do go somewhere. I wish I could have parents like Jessica has!"

- "Adam has been my best friend since we were in kindergarten. Now, though, I would rather hang out with Max. He and I like all the same things, and Max is the most popular kid in class. I want Adam to leave me alone."

Relationships

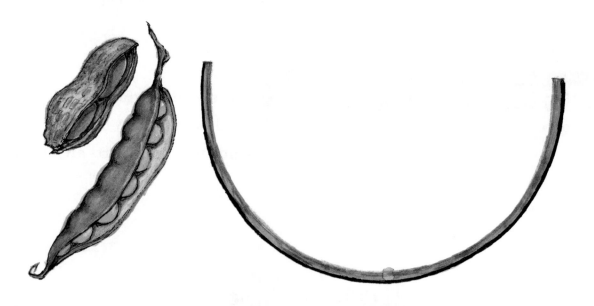

Review

Relationships: Your connection to, interactions with, and associations with other people.

Half-hearted

SOLOMON PRAYED FOR WISDOM.

SOLOMON BUILT A GLORIOUS TEMPLE.

1 KINGS 11:1–9

Whole-hearted

PSALM 9:1

PSALM 119:2

PSALM 86:12

Remember

"I have learned in whatever situation I am to be content." (Philippians 4:11)
(Also read verses 12–13.)

What does God say of all these commandments?

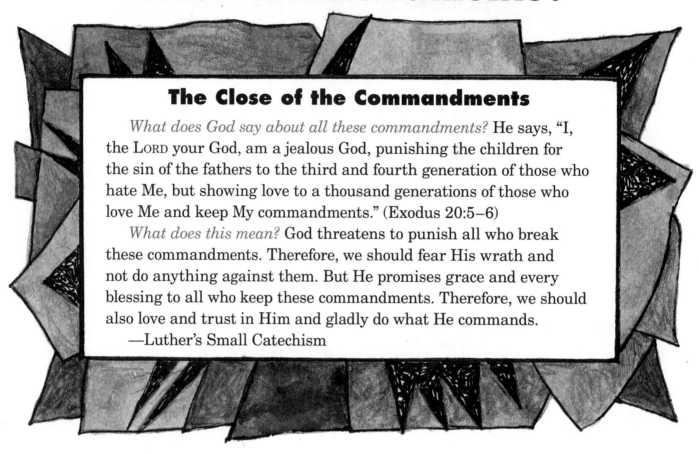

The Close of the Commandments

What does God say about all these commandments? He says, "I, the LORD your God, am a jealous God, punishing the children for the sin of the fathers to the third and fourth generation of those who hate Me, but showing love to a thousand generations of those who love Me and keep My commandments." (Exodus 20:5–6)

What does this mean? God threatens to punish all who break these commandments. Therefore, we should fear His wrath and not do anything against them. But He promises grace and every blessing to all who keep these commandments. Therefore, we should also love and trust in Him and gladly do what He commands.

—Luther's Small Catechism

Take This Seriously!

GOD EXPECTS US TO BE HOLY.

GOD HATES SIN.

HE WILL PUNISH SIN.

THERE ARE CONSEQUENCES TO SIN.

Review

Lemon: *(idiom)* imperfect, unsatisfactory, defective, doesn't work like it should, inadequate, worthless, failure.

We Are Lemons

Have you heard the old saying about turning lemons into lemonade? It means "taking something bad and turning it into something good." That is what God has done with us. Write your name on the lemon pictured here. How did God change you—imperfect, defective, and worthless—into

something good? _____

_____

_____

To represent this, draw a cross on the glass of lemonade and fill it with words that tell of the sweet blessings we have through Jesus, our Savior and Redeemer.

"How sweet are Your words to my taste, sweeter than honey to my mouth!" (Psalm 119:103)

"Oh, taste and see that the LORD is good!" (Psalm 34:8)

"I will bless the LORD at all times; His praise shall continually be in my mouth." (Psalm 34:1)

Who Am I?

1. In 2 Samuel 7:18, David had just been crowned king and the ark of the covenant had been returned to Jerusalem. David knew who God is, but now he asks, "Who am I?"

   What does he mean by this question? _____

   _____

2. David gave thanks for what good thing, promised by God (2 Samuel 7:16) to David and

   his house (family)? (See 2 Samuel 7:28–29.) _____

   _____

3. What do you know about this Son of David from Luke 2:4–7; Matthew 21:9–11;

   Matthew 27:35–37, 54; Matthew 28:5-7; Revelation 5:11–13? _____

   _____

Remember

"You shall be holy, for I the LORD your God am holy." (Leviticus 19:2)
"You, who once were alienated and hostile in mind, doing evil deeds, He has now reconciled in His body of flesh by His death, in order to present you holy and blameless and above reproach before Him."

(Colossians 1:21–22)

What do Law and Gospel mean for my life?

Three Mirrors

CONDEMNED

JUSTIFIED

SANCTIFIED

Cause and Effects

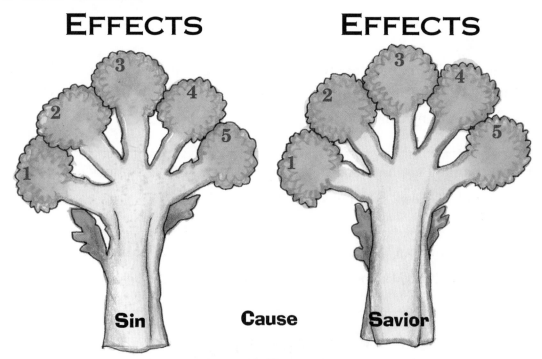

EFFECTS

EFFECTS

Sin   Cause   Savior

Review

Circle words related to the Law in blue; circle words related to the Gospel in red.

Grace	Demands	Condemns	Love	Mercy	Don't	Forgive
Guilty	Saved	Punishment	Redeemed	Death	Life	

Psalm 51:1–17

Circle the words in the psalm on the left that answer a question on the right. Connect the words and the question with an arrow.

PLEADING FOR FORGIVENESS

Have mercy on me, O God, according to Your steadfast love;
according to Your abundant mercy blot out my transgressions.

Wash me thoroughly from my iniquity, and cleanse me from my sin!

THE CONFESSION

For I know my transgressions, and my sin is ever before me.

Against You, You only, have I sinned and done what is evil in Your sight,
so that You may be justified in Your words and blameless in Your
judgment.

Behold, I was brought forth in iniquity, and in sin did my mother conceive
me.

PRAYER FOR A CHANGE OF HEART

Behold, You delight in truth in the inward being, and You teach me wisdom
in the secret heart.
Purge me with hyssop, and I shall be clean; wash me, and I shall be whiter
than snow.
Let me hear joy and gladness; let the bones that You have broken rejoice.
Hide Your face from my sins, and blot out all my iniquities.
Create in me a clean heart, O God, and renew a right spirit within me.
Cast me not away from Your presence, and take not Your Holy Spirit from
me.
Restore to me the joy of Your salvation, and uphold me with a willing spirit.

PRAYER FOR A CHANGE OF LIFE

Then I will teach transgressors Your ways, and sinners will return to You.
Deliver me from bloodguiltiness, O God, O God of my salvation,
and my tongue will sing aloud of Your righteousness.

O Lord, open my lips, and my mouth will declare Your praise.
For You will not delight in sacrifice, or I would give it;
You will not be pleased with a burnt offering.

The sacrifices of God are a broken spirit;
a broken and contrite heart, O God, You will not despise.

1. What words describe God's grace?

2. What words describe wrongdoing

3. What words show David is bothered by his sin?

4. What words remind us that all sin is against God?

5. What words refer to our sinful nature?

6. What words describe forgiveness?

7. What is the result of forgiveness?

8. How will David serve the Lord?

9. What does God want more than sacrifices?

Remember

Choose a verse from Psalm 51:1–17 to memorize. Highlight it in yellow above.

What does God's Word mean for my life?

What Is This?

Is this a modern-art oil painting? Is it a simple map? It is neither; it demonstrates a sad, sad story. This is the story of a man who followed God's path for a while and then took a wrong turn—a seriously wrong turn—and never got back on the right path. God's path leads to eternal life. Let's look at 2 Chronicles 24 to find out more about the misguided path.

Enoch (Genesis 5:22–24)

Λcll cc ʌ˙˙ղ Cᴖc

Review

Faithful: *(synonyms)* Loyal, trustworthy, constant, devoted, dutiful, reliable, genuine, dependable, honest, upright, honorable, unswerving, unwavering, enduring, unchanging, steady, dedicated, steadfast, sincere, conscientious. *God is faithful; He enables believers to become faithful.*

_____ Walks with God

How can you use each of these to either serve others, show kindness, or glorify God? Write your answers on the path that leads away from each picture.

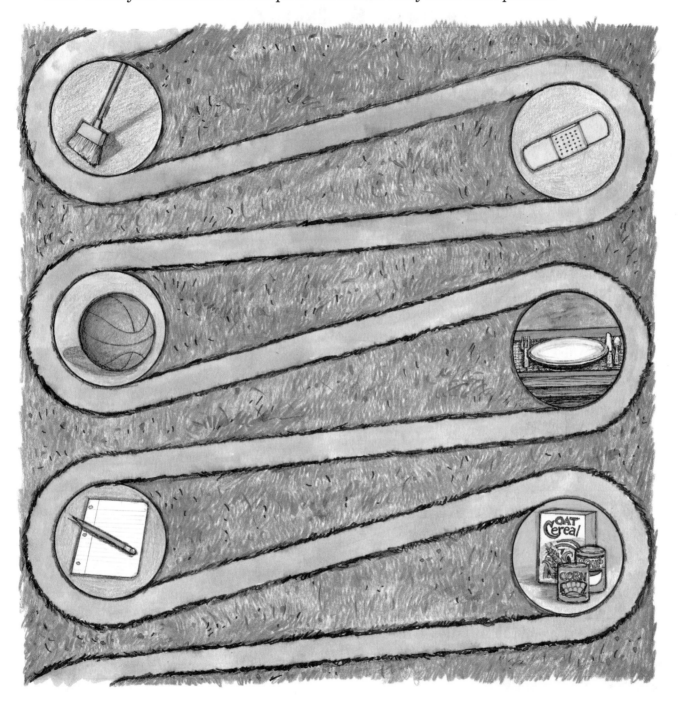

Remember

"By this we know that we abide in Him and He in us,* because He has given us of His Spirit." (1 John 4:13)

*Verse 15: "Whoever confesses that Jesus is the Son of God, God abides in him, and he in God."

What does it mean to live as God's child?

Team Member!

Wearing a uniform doesn't make you a member of a baseball team. Wearing the name *Christian* doesn't make you a team member, either. How do you get to be a part of God's team? _____

_____

_____

Good News: No one can take this from you. Jesus died so you are justified. It is complete.

Now what?

Good News: The Holy Spirit is transforming you to make you sanctified. It is continuing.

God's working in my life!

Goals

1. Eternal Life. Read 1 Corinthians 15:57 and comment on this goal. _____

_____

2. "Gwimyl" leads us to _____ and

_____

(See 2 Peter 3:18; 1 Thessalonians 3:12.)

3. My response to all Jesus has done for me is to " _____ _____ _____ _____

_____ , _____ , and _____." (See the explanation of the

Second Article of the Apostles' Creed.)

Expectations

Being people of God, just like being a team member, involves expectations. Rather than looking at these as rules or laws, we see expectations as *what we do because of who we are.* See Section 3 of Luther's Small Catechism for a Table of Duties—a list of responsibilities and expectations. Remember, you are not on your own: Gwimyl!

Review

> **Epistle**: A letter; often meaning the letters in the Bible written by an apostle.

Daily Workout

Diet. A coach will tell you that both diet and exercise are important parts of a daily workout program. What goes into you can energize and strengthen you. (But "garbage in" leads to "garbage out.") In our hearts, the Holy Spirit comes into us to energize and strengthen us in faith. We see in Galatians 5:22–23 what will then develop in our lives. Write your assigned word: _____ Tell what it means and tell what it looks or acts like in a person's life. _____

_____

_____

Exercise. Once again, we have a three-part plan.

1. Equipment. We are equipped through the Means of Grace, which are _____

_____ .

2. Practice. We need daily practice in serving God and other people.

How can you serve God? _____

_____

_____

How can you serve other people? _____

_____

_____

3. Support. Read Romans 15:4–5 and write ways you can receive and give support

(encouragement). _____

_____

_____

Yeah, Team!

Look around at your classmates, your family, and people in your church—these are your team members! Celebrate by singing "Kids of the Kingdom" (*AGPS* 150). Then look at the apostle Paul's words in Colossians, which encourage his (and our) teammates (fellow Christians).

Remember

"He has delivered us from the domain of darkness and transferred us to the kingdom of His beloved Son." (Colossians 1:13)

191

What blessings does God provide through my local congregation?

Jerusalem's Congregation

Problem: The pastors couldn't/shouldn't do it all (Acts 6:1–7).

Solution:

| Stephen | Philip | Prochorus | Nicanor | Timon | Parmenas | Nicolaus |

Characteristics (v. 3): _____

Our Local Congregation

Name: _____

Age: _____   Number of Members: _____

Employs _____ professional church workers and _____ support workers

Facilities: _____

_____

_____

_____

History: _____

_____

_____

_____

Review

These definitions are very similar. What small differences make each unique in how it is used?

Collaboration: to work together in a joint intellectual effort.

Cooperation: to act together toward a common purpose.

Coordination: to make harmonious adjustments and interactions.

My Congregation

☐ For grown-ups ☐ For me ☐ For _____

WHY GATHER?	**MY PLAN:**
• To worship together • To learn together • To work together • To encourage one another • To support one another	_____ _____ _____ _____

Concordia

Concordia means "harmony." God desires that His people, the Church, live in harmony. Because the Church consists of sinners, it sometimes has *discord*—harsh, disrupting clashes. We pray for God's forgiveness and for the gift of *concord,* which blends, builds, and brings peace. In these Scripture verses, highlight the key words that speak of God's will for the Church.

"We may be mutually encouraged by each other's faith, both yours and mine" (Romans 1:12).

"Rejoice with those who rejoice, weep with those who weep. Live in harmony with one another" (Romans 12:15–16).

"Live in such harmony with one another, in accord with Christ Jesus, that together you may with one voice glorify the God and Father of our Lord Jesus Christ" (Romans 15:5–6).

"Maintain the unity of the Spirit in the bond of peace . . . one Lord, one faith, one baptism, one God and Father of all, who is over all and through all and in all" (Ephesians 4:3, 5).

"Equip the saints for the work of ministry, for building up the body of Christ, until we all attain to the unity of the faith and of the knowledge of the Son of God" (Ephesians 4:12–13).

"Therefore we ought to support people like these, that we may be fellow workers for the truth" (3 John 8).

"Oh, magnify the LORD with me, and let us exalt His name together!" (Psalm 34:3).

"Therefore encourage one another and build one another up" (1 Thessalonians 5:11).

"Finally, all of you, have unity of mind, sympathy, brotherly love, a tender heart, and a humble mind" (1 Peter 3:8).

Remember

"Above all these put on love, which binds everything together in perfect harmony." (Colossians 3:14)

What blessings does God provide through my church organization?

Our Lutheran Identity

Lutheran Church—Missouri Synod

Synod: organization assembly committee meeting conference congress gathering walking together partnership family

We Believe

B_____

B_____

C_____

C_____

We Share

_____

_____

and More!

Review

Organization: People or groups working together for a united purpose.

Identity: The characteristics by which something is specifically recognized or known.

We Care

The LCMS has and partners with many organizations that serve many specific purposes to care and share God's loving kindness with people who have a variety of needs. Match the name of each organization with its acronym.

___ 1. OGT

a. Lutheran Women's Missionary League

___ 2. LBW

b. Lutheran Laymen's League

___ 3. LLL

c. Lutheran Bible Translators

___ 4. OAFC

d. World Relief and Human Care

___ 5. CGO

e. Orphan Grain Train

___ 6. LAMP

f. Ongoing Ambassadors for Christ

___ 7. WRHC

g. The Apple of His Eye Mission Society

___ 8. LCEF

h. Bethesda Lutheran Home and Services

___ 9. AHEM

i. Lutheran Braille Workers

___ 10. LWML

j. Concordia Gospel Outreach

___ 11. BLHS

k. Lutheran Association of Missionaries and Pilots (US)

___ 12. LBT

l. Lutheran Church Extension Fund

LCMS

Remember

"Blessed . . . are those who hear the word of God and keep it!"
(Luke 11:28)

How does Christian education bless us?

Jesus' Teachers

1. In Bible times, parents were the first teachers of children. The same is true today! Read Deuteronomy 6:4–7. What does verse 7 tell parents to do? _____

   _____

   _____

2. As we've learned, there is strength in numbers. Also, different people have different abilities and can teach us different things. Jesus most likely attended a synagogue school, as did other boys at that time. We also know that He studied with rabbis in the temple. Who are some of the people you learn from? _____

   _____

3. Read about Jesus in Luke 2:41–52 when He was about your age. Then look again at verses 46 and 52. These are probably the most significant verses in this familiar story. What did you learn from those verses? Why are they important to you? _____

   _____

   _____

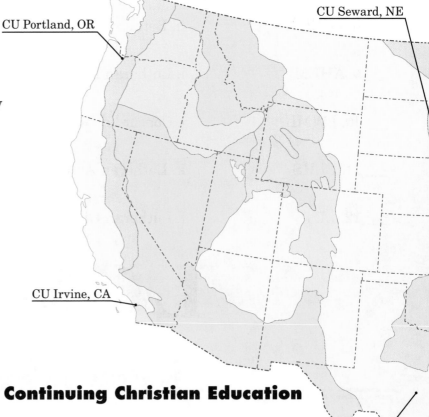

KEY:
CU = Concordia University
CC = Concordia College
SEM = Seminary

CU Portland, OR

CU Seward, NE

CU Irvine, CA

Review

Synagogue: _____

_____

_____

_____

_____

_____

_____

Continuing Christian Education

CU Austin, TX

My Teachers

As a class, interview your teacher. Here are possible questions to ask: Why did you decide to become a teacher at a Christian school? Where did you get your college education? Where have you taught and what have you taught? What is your favorite thing about teaching? In the box, make notes about questions of your own. On the lines, write what you learned about your teacher.

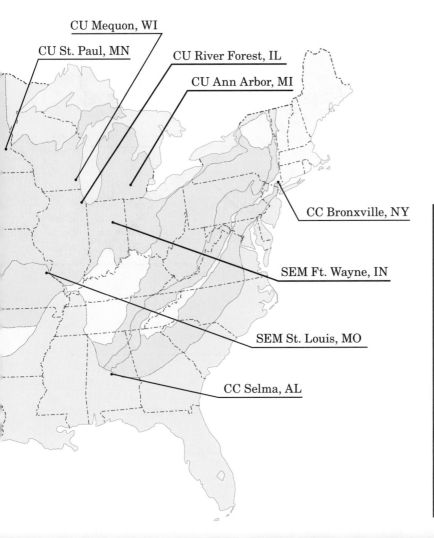

CU Mequon, WI

CU St. Paul, MN

CU River Forest, IL

CU Ann Arbor, MI

CC Bronxville, NY

SEM Ft. Wayne, IN

SEM St. Louis, MO

CC Selma, AL

Remember

"Continue in what you have learned and have firmly believed, knowing from whom you learned it and how from childhood you have been acquainted with the sacred writings, which are able to make you wise for salvation through faith in Christ Jesus."

(2 Timothy 3:14–15)

197

How can I witness to my friends and the members of my family?

Witness Targets

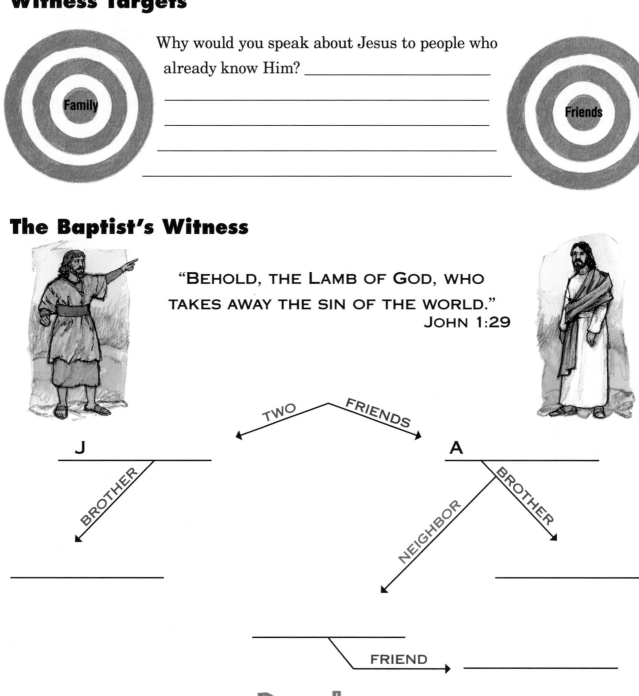

Why would you speak about Jesus to people who already know Him? _____

_____

_____

_____

Family

Friends

The Baptist's Witness

"BEHOLD, THE LAMB OF GOD, WHO TAKES AWAY THE SIN OF THE WORLD."
JOHN 1:29

TWO FRIENDS

J _____   A _____

BROTHER

NEIGHBOR   BROTHER

_____   _____

_____

FRIEND   _____

Review

Witness: _____

Opportunity: _____

Witness? Where?

Ways to Witness: _____

_____

_____

_____

_____

Ways to Witness: _____

_____

_____

_____

_____

Comments

Remember

"In your _____ _____ Christ the Lord as holy, always being

_____ to make a _____ to anyone who asks you for a _____

for the _____ that is in you; yet do it with _____ and

_____." (1 Peter 3:15)

How can I witness to those who don't care?

The Sad Case of Agrippa

The *sad case* of Agrippa? He was a wealthy and powerful king! It's the apostle Paul who looks like a *sad case*—arrested and in chains. Let's discover what was so sad about Agrippa.

1. Why was Paul arrested (Acts 21:31–33)? _____

_____

2. Why did Felix keep Paul in prison (Acts 24:26)? _____

_____

_____

3. Why was Paul still in prison after two years when

the new governor Festus arrived (Acts 24:27)? _____

4. Why was Paul brought before King Agrippa (Acts 25:24–27)? _____

_____

5. What was Paul's message (Acts 26:22–23)? _____

_____

6. What was Agrippa's response (Acts 26:28–29)? Why is this sad? _____

_____

It Takes Courage

Paul was beaten and imprisoned for speaking about the loving grace of Jesus, the Savior. Our situations today are very different than his. And yet it still takes courage to share the love of God. Why

does this take courage in our lives today? _____

_____

_____

"Be strong and courageous. Do not be frightened, and do not be dismayed, for the LORD your God is with you wherever you go." (Joshua 1:9)

"Wait for the Lord; be strong, and let your heart take courage; wait for the Lord!" (Psalm 27:14)

Review

Opportunity: A fortunate possibility; a convenient time. *The apostle Paul considered his trials an opportunity to speak about the loving grace of Jesus. King Agrippa lost the opportunity of knowledge of eternal salvation because he wasn't interested.*

Whatever . . .

Whatever can be a very sad word. Often the person saying it means "I just don't care." When you are trying to share God's love or God's forgiveness, it can be sad to hear someone respond, "Whatever." The problem is that *you do care*, even if they don't. You care about God and you care about the person who doesn't care! When facing problems like this, here are things to think about. As your teacher reads a list of words, write down an example or description of the first thing you think of.

1. _____   5. _____

2. _____   6. _____

3. _____   7. _____

4. _____   8. _____

Don't Be Discouraged

God desires that we share His love, forgiveness, and message of salvation through Christ Jesus. But if someone doesn't listen or doesn't care, don't be discouraged. It is not your responsibility and it's not even your ability to create faith. That is the work of the Holy Spirit. (Write out the Scripture verses.)

> 1 Corinthians 12:3 "No one can _____
> _____."

The Holy Spirit works through the Means of Grace. The Holy Spirit uses you as a tool.

> Acts 9:15 "He is a _____
> _____."

Rely on the blessings of the Holy Spirit to guide what you say and do.

> John 14:26 "The Holy Spirit, _____
> _____."

Remember

"My God will supply every need of yours according to His riches in glory in Christ Jesus." (Philippians 4:19)

201

How can I witness to those who ridicule and oppose me?

Four Responses

Jesus suffered much to take away our sins and make us children of God. But it is not easy to live as a child of God. Many people say, "It is easier for me to do whatever I want. It is easier to follow along with whatever my friends want to do. It is easier to do what everyone else is doing." It is true—it is not easy being a Christian. There may be times when people will reject you, ridicule you, and even harm you for following Jesus' ways. How can you respond? Four possibilities are listed below. Match those responses to what happened in each of these stories.

_____ 1. Monica knew what the other girls were planning to do. Nobody in the class liked the new girl—she seemed so shy and afraid. Monica sat on a bench and watched as the other girls set up their plan. Two people out of sight held the ends of a rope while a third person gave the signal when the new girl came near. Trip! Books flew! People laughed! It happened exactly as Monica expected it would.

_____ 2. Tyler was glad that his older cousins came over to play until they started throwing rocks at the neighbor's cats. "Come on, Tyler," yelled his cousin Kelvin. "Don't worry, your neighbors aren't home, so they won't catch us. Or are you too much of a goody-goody to play with us?" Tyler didn't like to be teased, so he picked up a handful of rocks and began using his hardest pitch on the cats.

_____ 3. A group of boys made a plan to go into the Big Mart to see who could shoplift the most valuable item. Fletcher said, "No way. That's a sin." Ahkeem shoved Fletcher and called him chicken-livered. Fletcher shoved back and said, "You're just a loudmouth, Ahkeem." Then Fletcher punched Ahkeem in the face.

_____ 4. Mr. Johnson announced that he had to go to a funeral that afternoon, so the class would have a substitute teacher. Over lunch break, the kids began planning simple ways to make the sub's life miserable, like having all the boys switch their nametags with the girls. Olivia listened and then said, "Stop it, guys. This is a Christian school. Let's act like Christians." Andrew joined in and said, "Olivia is right. What message would we be giving the sub about our school and about us as God's people? Let's really surprise her and be cooperative and kind!"

Responses

a. **Join with:** To abandon Jesus by joining with the others in their sinful actions.
b. **Stand back:** To protect yourself by saying or doing nothing, as if you didn't care.
c. **Pulled in:** Fighting back against those doing wrong, returning their bad behavior.
d. **Stand up:** Speaking the truth about God's ways and defending what is right.

Jesus' Response

See Jesus' response in Luke 4 when people became angry and wanted to harm Him.

1. Jesus was just beginning His ministry. He was preaching in what area (v. 14)? _____
   How did the people react to Him (v. 15)? _____

2. Jesus went to Nazareth, which was _____ (vv. 16, 23).
   What did they ask Jesus to do (vv. 16–21)? _____
   _____ This was customary to ask of a teacher or rabbi like Jesus.

3. Read verses 22–27. At first, the people spoke well of Jesus. But then some began to question who He was because He was just a carpenter's son. Others wanted to see Him do miracles as He had in other places. And then they really became angry when Jesus compared Himself to the prophets Elijah and Elisha, who spoke also to the Gentiles, and He compared the people of Nazareth to the people who had rejected the prophets. What did the people of Nazareth want to do now (vv. 28–29)? _____
   _____

4. What was Jesus' response (v. 30)? _____
   In what way are Jesus' words in Matthew 10:14 similar? _____
   _____

Spiritual Warfare

Jesus has won the victory for us. However, as long as we are on this earth, there will be daily battles against sin and evil. Those are the enemies we fight daily. We sing about this in hymns such as "Lift High the Cross" and "Onward, Christian Soldiers." We must be careful, though, to not make these mistakes about spiritual warfare:

> **Misunderstanding #1.** Some people think this is a physical battle. It is not. We do not fight with a **SWORD**. We fight sin, temptation, and evil with the **SWORD**. (Correct the last word by scribbling off one letter; see Ephesians 6:17.)

> **Misunderstanding #2.** Some people act as if the term "spiritual warfare" means fighting and arguing with other Christians. However, Scripture calls on us to support and encourage fellow Christians, as Galatians 6:10 states, "So then, as we have opportunity, let us do good to everyone, and *especially to those who are of the household of faith*" (emphasis added).

Remember

> "Be strong in the Lord and in the strength of His might."
>
> (Ephesians 6:10)

Who is the true God?

Proclaimed from Mars Hill

(Acts 17:16–34)

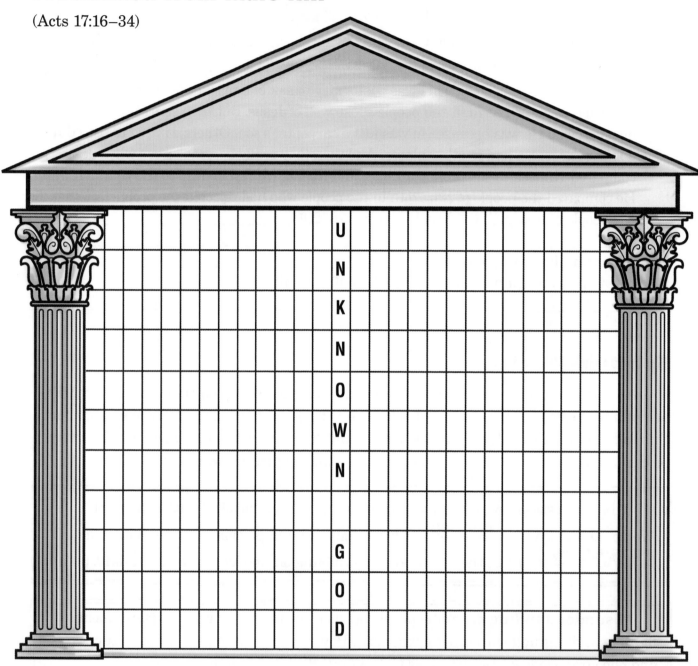

U
N
K
N
O
W
N

G
O
D

Directions: You know the true God and what He is like! Above, write words and phrases about the Lord, incorporating the printed letters.

Review

Charity: (1) Kindness shown, especially to those in need. (2) Love; *In older translations of 1 Corinthians 13, the word love has been translated as charity.*

God Is Love!

The main difference between other religions and Christianity is the difference between fear and love. We do not need to be afraid of being punished for doing wrong and we do not need to be afraid we won't do enough good to get to heaven. Jesus loves us and has taken care of all this for us! Jesus died on the cross and arose at Easter and gives the victory to us—because of His great love. Love is what is unique about faith in Jesus. God loves us and leads us to show love—by loving God in return and sharing loving kindness with others. Use 1 Corinthians 13 to complete this section from the great "love chapter."

♡ ♡ ♡ ♡ ♡ ♡ ♡ ♡ ♡ ♡ ♡ ♡ ♡ ♡ ♡ ♡ ♡

From 1 Corinthians 13

Verse 4:

Love is _____.

Love is _____.

It does not _____.

It does not _____.

It is not _____.

Verse 5:

It is not _____.

It does not _____.

It is not _____.

It is not _____.

Verse 6:

It does not _____.

But _____.

Verse 7:

Love _____.

Love _____.

Love _____.

Love _____.

Verse 8:

Love never _____.

Verse 13:

So now _____

_____

_____

_____.

♡ ♡ ♡ ♡ ♡ ♡ ♡ ♡ ♡ ♡ ♡ ♡ ♡ ♡ ♡ ♡ ♡

Remember

"And there is salvation in no one else, for there is no other name under heaven given among men by which we must be saved." (Acts 4:12)

Whose name is this talking about? Check the context by reading verses 10–11.

205

A new you? A new me?

Your Job as a Treasurer

Scripture says, "If anyone is in Christ, he is a new creation" (2 Corinthians 5:17). So, what is your life like as a new person? There is a new you and that "new you" is a treasurer! What are the riches of this treasure? (Read Romans 11:33; Ephesians 1:7; 2:7; Colossians 1:27; 2:2–3.) _____

_____

_____

It's a treasure no one can take away!

It's a treasure you can give away and still keep!

What are you supposed to do with this treasure? (It's your job as treasurer!)

_____

_____

_____

Review

Treasurer: Someone in charge of the receipt, care, and disbursement of something valuable; trustee; steward.

Ambassador: Representative of someone.

Your Job as an Ambassador

Job Description

An ambassador is a very significant role. The ambassador represents another person or group. The ambassador stands in for, acts in place of, or speaks for the person represented. The ambassador shares similar opinions with and communicates messages from the one represented. The ambassador needs to be an example of, typical of, an imitation of, and an embodiment of those represented.

As new creations in Christ, we are to be His ambassadors! What an honor and privilege to live for Him! But how can we sinners possibly do this? (See 1 Corinthians 6:11.) _____

_____

_____

In what ways can you be an ambassador for Christ? _____

_____

_____

What message are you to communicate as an ambassador for Christ? (See 1 Corinthians 13:13; 15:3.) _____

_____

_____

Remember

"For I am sure that neither death nor life, nor angels nor rulers, nor things present nor things to come, nor powers, nor height nor depth, nor anything else in all creation, will be able to separate us from the love of God in Christ Jesus our Lord." (Romans 8:38–39)

APPENDIX

Table of Contents

Books of the Bible
(Sixty-Six Books)

Old Testament
(Thirty-Nine Books)

Genesis: This is a book of beginnings—the beginning of the world, the beginning of sin, and the beginning of God's promise to Adam and Eve to send a Savior to rescue humankind from sin and death. Because of the extent of sin, God makes a new beginning by sending the great flood and starting anew with Noah and his family. But sin remains, and God chooses a family to build into a nation that will carry the promise of the Messiah—the only salvation from sin. God gives this promise to Abraham, who passes it on to his family through Isaac, Jacob, Judah, and so on. As in the story of Joseph, we see that even when all around us seems to go wrong, God has a plan to give us hope and blessing.

Exodus: The story of God's chosen people—known then as the Hebrews or Israelites—continues in the Book of Exodus, which means to go out. The people go out of slavery in Egypt, led by the Lord and His appointed leader, Moses. This is a story of God's faithfulness, patience, and blessing to a people who, like us, are undeserving and continue to fall into sin. God's grace and forgiveness are constant as He leads them to the Promised Land.

Leviticus: Leviticus is the third of the five books known as the Pentateuch (which are also known as the Books of Moses and the Books of the Law). Leviticus focuses on God's people as a special people set apart to worship Him and to live through obedience, rededicating their lives to God's service. The sacrifices, feasts, and offerings foreshadow, or point to, the Messiah, Jesus, the perfect sacrifice to come; so, though this is called a Book of the Law, it also contains a Gospel message of hope through the promised Savior.

Numbers: The name of this book refers to the counting of people and property, but it is largely about the Israelites wandering in the desert wilderness. Time and again, we see God faithfully providing for His people. The mercy and grace of Jesus is foreshadowed through the account of the bronze snake (lifted up for God's promise of deliverance), the rock that brings saving water, and the daily manna. These are a preview of Jesus as the eternal living water and the bread of life eternal.

Deuteronomy: Deuteronomy is the retelling of God's law. This is a review of what God has done and of God's will for a new generation of people, preparing them for their life in the Promised Land. God calls His people to rededicate their lives to Him, reminding Israel again of the promise God has made to them and the promise they have made to Him in the covenant that He will be their God and they will be His people. We have this promise, too, in the new covenant, or New Testament, which we have through the work of Christ Jesus.

Joshua: This begins the Books of History, which continue through the Book of Esther. Joshua, meaning "the Lord is salvation," becomes the new leader, taking the people into the Promised Land (Canaan) after the death of Moses. Joshua calls on the people to remain faithful to God, who has always been faithful to them. Joshua foreshadows Jesus, who leads us to the promised land of heaven through His death and resurrection.

Judges: This Book of History tells of the ongoing cycle of people "doing what was right in their own eyes," turning away from God, falling under the power of evil enemies and tribulation, God's call to repentance, and God's deliverance through His chosen leaders (such as Gideon, Deborah, and Samson). This is a cycle that continues even today as God continues to call us to repentance from our sinfulness and as He offers deliverance from the evils of sin, death, and Satan through the salvation we have in Jesus. God's faithful love is constant.

Ruth: The story of Ruth is about a woman who was not an Israelite, but came to faith in God and became one of the ancestors of Jesus, reminding us that God's Kingdom is for all people who have faith in Him. The Book of Ruth examines the concept of redemption, or "buying back," which foreshadows Jesus as our Redeemer who bought us back from the power of the devil; the price was His own body and blood on the cross. The story of Ruth again shows the faithfulness of God in the midst of difficult circumstances in a changing world.

1 and 2 Samuel: The story of Samuel as prophet, priest, and judge foreshadows or previews Jesus, the greatest Prophet, Priest, and King! Up until the time of Samuel, leaders were chosen by God to carry out His will because God Himself was the true ruler of the people. In time, however, the people wanted a king like other nations around them. The first two kings, Saul and David, were anointed by God's prophet Samuel. Both of these kings were sinners, as are all people; but Saul turned away from God while David turned to God in repentance and received forgiveness. God made a wonderful promise to David that the Messiah, the King of kings, would come from his family. This promise is completed through Jesus (often called the Son of David), who rules forever as our Savior and who will someday take all believers to His kingdom in heaven.

1 and 2 Kings: These books are a continuation of the history found in 1 and 2 Samuel, from the time of the united kingdom (when David and Solomon ruled as kings) through the times of the divided kingdom (with Israel in the north and Judah in the south). The Northern Kingdom never had a king who was faithful to God; eventually, God allowed the Assyrians to capture and exile that nation. The Southern Kingdom of Judah was largely unfaithful, though occasionally, there were God-fearing kings who tried to lead the people back to the Lord. But eventually, Judah, too, was taken into captivity, in exile in Babylon. Throughout these years of turmoil, God continued the royal line of David in Judah and maintained the promise of the Messiah to come. God continued to send His words of Law and Gospel through the prophets, whose writings are found in the latter portion of the Old Testament.

1 and 2 Chronicles: These books focus on the reigns of King David and his son Solomon (who built the temple), continuing on through their royal family line in the Southern Kingdom. This family line also carried the promise of the Messiah, who came centuries later in the fullness of time in Christ Jesus. The author of Chronicles reminds the people that God has cared for them in the past and His care will continue throughout the ages. Leaders and governments change, but God remains unchanging in His call to repentance, grace, and mercy.

Ezra: The books of Ezra, Nehemiah, and Esther continue the story of God's people who had been in captivity in Babylon for seventy years and who finally began to see their need for reliance and hope in the true God. Ezra was part of a group who returned to Jerusalem to complete the rebuilding of the temple, assuring the people that God continued to be present with them. Ezra, a priest, taught the people God's Word and prayed for their forgiveness and renewed faithfulness. God kept alive the promise of the Savior, who was to be born in the land of Judah.

Nehemiah: God worked through Ezra to rebuild His people spiritually; God worked through Nehemiah to rebuild His people physically. Without the protection of city walls, the people who had returned to Jerusalem from captivity were in constant danger. God answered Nehemiah's prayers, choosing him to guide the people to rebuild the walls in just fifty-two days, using armed guards working side by side with the construction workers to protect the project. At the dedication of the wall, the people gave all glory to God!

Esther: This is the story of Jewish people who stayed in Persia instead of returning to Judah. Again, we see how God can work through ordinary people, such as Esther, to accomplish His will. Through God's plan, Esther, though Jewish, became a queen in Persia and bravely spoke up for her people, even at the risk of her own life. We see again that God is with His people blessing them and working through them to make a difference. This ends the historical section of the Old Testament.

Job: This begins the section of five books called Wisdom and Poetry. These were originally written in Hebrew and do not rhyme as many poems in English do. (Hebrew poetry repeats ideas rather than repeating sounds.) This is the story of a man who loses everything and suffers much. Through his story, we learn that the devil, not God, is actually responsible for sufferings, but God is in control and limits how much Satan may do. We cannot always understand God's wisdom and loving plans, but He is always with us, working to accomplish His good purpose. Job's life is a witness to others that even troubles can provide opportunities to praise God. God heard Job's pleas in his time of trouble and restored Job to health and gave him many new blessings. One of the clearest Old Testament passages on resurrection is in chapter 19, where Job says, "I know that my Redeemer lives."

Psalms: The Book of Psalms is sometimes called the hymnal of the Old Testament—a book of prayer and praise. Psalms gives us examples of how God's people deal with both joys and sorrows. The psalms express the personal relationship that believers have with their God. David (as shepherd, warrior, and king) wrote about half of the psalms. This book repeats the theme that God is the good and faithful King of all creation and to His people. There are also frequent references to the coming Messiah.

Proverbs: This is a collection of wise sayings that tell us how to live a godly life. There is practical advice on many subjects, such as making friends, handling money, and caring for the poor. But real wisdom is based on honoring and faithfully following God. Proverbs appears to be very law oriented, telling you what to do and not do. However, a repentant sinner, justified through Christ Jesus, can look at these verses as guidelines for living a sanctified life through the enabling power of the Holy Spirit.

Ecclesiastes: The author of this book directs us to the real purpose of life and encourages us to stay away from things that are meaningless. Some things in life are empty, but life with God brings true joy and direction. Fame, possessions, power, and wealth cannot bring the eternal blessings of forgiveness, life, and salvation, which we receive only through Christ Jesus.

Song of Solomon: Also known as Song of Songs, this book tells of the relationship between a husband and wife and, in turn, illustrates the love God has for us. God's love is perfect, faithful, and He wants us with Him always. This is a love that is willing to give up everything for the loved one, which is what Jesus did when He gave up His life for our salvation.

Isaiah: The remainder of the Old Testament contains the books of the prophets: the first five are considered the Major Prophets, and the next twelve are the Minor Prophets. The prophets spoke messages from God, mostly during the time of the divided kingdom, but with words that are still significant in today's world. They spoke warnings about sin, pleaded for repentance, and continued to give more information about the coming of the Messiah. Although Isaiah lived centuries before Christ, he told how Jesus would be born, suffer, die, and rise again to take away our sins. God's promises of the Messiah comforted His people, even when Judah was in misery because of sin. The prophets Amos, Hosea, and Micah were also living at this time.

Jeremiah: Jeremiah loved his Lord; He also loved his nation enough to speak out the truth about its sin and the coming consequences. Jeremiah dramatically called the people to repent and spoke compassionately of God's forgiveness, mercy, and the promise of the Savior—the Lord, "our Righteousness"—who was yet to come. His harsh warnings often made him unpopular with his countrymen, who ridiculed and even hated him. Although many people did not consider Jeremiah to be successful in changing the hearts of the people, he was truly successful in that he faithfully and boldly proclaimed God's Word.

Lamentations: Lamentations is a poetic book of weeping. The author, thought to be Jeremiah, is crying over the destruction of Jerusalem—the consequence of sin, as prophesied. However, even in the middle of terrible sadness, with God there is hope. God's compassion never fails. God did later restore His people, and through them, He kept His promise of the Messiah.

Ezekiel: The prophet Ezekiel lived in the time when Jerusalem had been conquered and the temple burned. In the middle of these difficult times, God chose Ezekiel to call the people to repentance and to restore and renew them spiritually. Ezekiel used picture language and even acted out some of his prophecies to explain the visions he had received from the Lord, telling of God's grace and mercy.

Daniel: The Book of Daniel is partly narrative story and partly visionary prophecy. Though Daniel and his friends are in exile in a foreign country, God blesses their faithfulness and bold witness in amazing ways. The book emphasizes that God is the ruler over all kingdoms and His reign is forever. The latter half of the book records amazing visions Daniel received from God about the future, and particularly about the coming Messiah. God is in charge of all history, and He directs all things for the purpose of saving His people through Christ Jesus.

Hosea: This is the first book of the Minor Prophets. It tells of the prophet Hosea's relationship to his unfaithful wife Gomer. Hosea's life becomes a picture or symbol of God's constant, continual love for His people. Even when they are unfaithful to Him, God continues to call His people to repentance. Unlike most prophets, who were from Judah, Hosea was from the Northern Kingdom of Israel.

Joel: This prophet speaks of the destruction in Judah recently caused by a swarm of locusts that destroyed the crops as God's punishment for sin. Joel warns that if the people do not repent, there will be even greater destruction, caused by the swarm of an enemy's army. He says that the Day of the Lord will come to punish sin, but those who trust in God will be saved. God still promises salvation to all who trust Him, in Jesus.

Amos: Amos was a shepherd who became God's prophet to warn the people at a time of great wealth and idolatry. He warned the people not to trust in money or images, but to trust in the true God. Though the message is of condemnation, the book ends with a word of hope in the continued promise of the Savior for all who believe.

Obadiah: Obadiah is the shortest book in the Old Testament. This prophet speaks against the people of Edom, who were glad to see Judah suffering when taken captive by Babylon and rejoiced and benefited from Judah's despair. The prophet repeats God's promises to one day restore His people to their land.

Jonah: Jonah was an unwilling prophet who tried to run from God's command. He did not want God's message of repentance and forgiveness to be shared with the people of Nineveh, Israel's Assyrian enemy. God clearly wants all people to hear His Word and to come to faith—a message for us today to share with all people. Centuries later, Jesus compared His burial in the tomb and resurrection on the third day to Jonah's three days in the belly of the great fish.

Micah: The Book of Micah explains that God hates sin but loves the sinner. Though the people would be punished for their refusal to repent of sin, the prophet also speaks a message of hope in the coming Messiah. Micah points to Bethlehem as the birthplace of the Savior, who would care for His sheep and lead them like a shepherd. Though the people would still have to wait centuries for the fullness of time, God kept these promises in Christ Jesus, who, as Micah prophesied, came with strength, majesty, greatness, and peace.

Nahum: About 150 years after the time of Jonah, the people of Nineveh in Assyria had returned to their wicked and idolatrous ways. Nahum pronounced God's judgment on this nation that had taken Israel captive. Nahum said that God is slow to anger, but He brings justice on those who are guilty and is a refuge in times of trouble for those who trust in Him.

Habakkuk: This is a conversation, as the prophet asks God many questions and God answers, revealing His plan. God assures us that we can hope in Him even when surrounded by troubles because He is still in control and His will will be done. The prophet concludes by saying, "I will take joy in the God of my salvation" (3:18).

Zephaniah: This book begins with sorrow over the sin of the people, but that sadness turns to joy as the prophet speaks of God's deliverance and salvation. God will lead the people to repentance so that He may then rejoice over them and gather them to Himself. The prophet says that when the people return to the Lord, He will bless them and through them the whole earth will be blessed. That blessing for all the earth is the promised Savior who will bring forgiveness and salvation to those who trust in the Lord.

Haggai: The prophet Haggai encouraged the people returning from captivity to Jerusalem in order to rebuild their temple, and he called them to action. While this temple would not be as beautiful as Solomon's, it would have greater glory in that the Savior would one day come to this new temple.

Zechariah: As Zechariah encourages the rebuilding of the temple, he gives even greater encouragement through specific prophecies about the promised Savior, foretelling Jesus' triumphant entry into Jerusalem on Palm Sunday, His being betrayed for thirty pieces of silver, and His cleansing away of sin by His blood.

Malachi: The last Old Testament prophet, Malachi, foretold of the messenger (John the Baptist) who would come and get people ready for the coming of the Messiah (Jesus). Malachi is a bridge between the Old and New Testaments, a time span of four hundred years.

New Testament
(Twenty-Seven books)

Matthew: The four Gospels tell the stories of Jesus' life, death, and resurrected life, each with a unique perspective. Matthew, writing to a largely Jewish audience, emphasized that Jesus indeed is the promised Messiah by making strong connections to the Old Testament. Matthew shows time and again how Jesus fulfilled the prophecies of old, specifically and completely. The book begins with a genealogy showing that Jesus came from the royal line of David, but then goes on to show Jesus as King of kings who brings salvation to all people.

Mark: The style of the Gospel of Mark is full of action about what Jesus did (rather than what He fulfilled). The primary audience was Roman Christians, who would appreciate this active style of writing, which is brief and to the point. Mark was an assistant to the disciple Peter (Mark's mentor and primary source of information).

Luke: The author of this book, Luke, was a doctor who followed a second career as a missionary and also as a writer. Luke emphasizes Jesus' compassion for people as he tells of Jesus' teachings (especially in parables) and also of the miracles in Jesus' healing ministry. Jesus' compassion for people includes the poor, humble, the unpopular, and even the outcasts. Luke's primary sources appear to be Mary (Jesus' mother) and also the apostle Paul, with whom he traveled on many missionary journeys. Luke wrote this Gospel—as well as the Book of Acts—to Theophilus, a Gentile.

John: John's viewpoint tends to be more philosophical than the other Gospels, focusing more on the teachings of Jesus. This would relate especially well to John's Greek audience. His constant theme is the love of Jesus for all people. John states the purpose of this book when he says, "that you may believe that Jesus is the Christ, the Son of God, and that by believing you may have life in His name" (20:31). John emphasizes that Jesus is God's Word in the flesh; we know God by knowing Jesus, who Himself is true God.

Acts: Luke wrote this book of history called the Acts of the Apostles (which could actually be called the Acts of the Holy Spirit). It tells of the early growth of the Christian Church from the time of Christ's ascension into heaven through the giving of the Holy Spirit at Pentecost and then to the spread of the Gospel throughout the world. Acts also tells how the Holy Spirit works in the lives of individual believers such as Stephen, Peter, Paul, Philip, Lydia, and Dorcas.

Romans: Romans through Philemon are the Pauline Epistles, letters written by the apostle Paul to Christian churches (nine letters) and individual believers (four letters). The Book of Romans was written to the Christian church in Rome around the time of the emperor Nero. This epistle gives an eloquent account of the basic details of our Christian faith as it emphasizes the grace and mercy that is a gift from God through Christ Jesus. The focus is on eternal salvation for all who believe that we are justified through Christ's death and resurrection for our forgiveness.

1 and 2 Corinthians: These epistles were written to people in the seaport city of Corinth, a city known for its many idols to false gods. Paul heard that the church in Corinth had many problems. He wrote these letters to encourage them to remove their divisions and to be united in teachings about salvation through Jesus. He wanted them to restore order as they celebrated the Lord's Supper and to show loving care to others, especially those in need. The message of these letters is clear, strong, and very direct to the people then as well as people today.

Galatians: Paul's Letter to the Galatians reminds the Christians there that they need to clearly separate Law and Gospel. Some of the people were demanding that new Christians follow old Jewish law. Paul emphasizes that faith in Jesus alone is all that is necessary for salvation, not rules or works. This letter was probably passed around to several churches in Galatia, which is part of modern-day Turkey.

Ephesians: Ephesus was a very large commercial city. In this letter, Paul emphasizes clearly the message of salvation by grace alone in Christ. Paul wants the church in Ephesus to understand that there is nothing they can do to earn salvation; it is a gift of God through faith created by the Holy Spirit. As Paul describes and directs the church in Ephesus, he is speaking to us today, too, that the church is not a building but believers in Christ Jesus who want to serve Him.

Philippians: Philippi was a wealthy Roman colony in Macedonia. This letter to the Philippian church was a thank-you note from Paul for the gift they had sent him. It is a letter full of joy and expresses the love that Paul had for them, encouraging them to be faithful and to be united as troubles come to them. Paul encouraged them to face hard times with joy, knowing that in Christ they could do all things.

Colossians: Paul wrote to the church in the city of Colossae that they should be careful of the false teachings that were challenging them. He wants them to know that human ideas are nothing compared to the greatness of God. Knowledge combined with other philosophies and religions does not bring saving truth. Paul encouraged people in this church to let their faith be shown in good works. Since Colossae was on an important trade route, information could easily be passed on from this church location to other churches.

1 and 2 Thessalonians: Thessalonica was a busy seaport that served as an important trade center. These epistles were written to Christians there that were under attack and physically persecuted. Paul encouraged the believers in Thessalonica to continue in their faith and look forward to the hope that is theirs in Christ Jesus. Paul also replied to their questions concerning the second coming of Christ, assuring them that this will not be a fearful time for believers, but rather a time of comfort and joy.

1 and 2 Timothy: Having been raised in a godly home, Timothy was led to Christ and trained by Paul as Timothy accompanied Paul on several mission trips. Paul wrote these two letters to Timothy to explain how church workers should teach and live. Paul also gives Timothy information on recognizing and dealing with false teachers. Paul is handing over his ministry to the church to a new generation as he challenges Timothy to put his hope and trust in the message of Christ Jesus.

Titus: This letter is to Titus, a Greek, who is a church worker on the island of Crete and had traveled with Paul on some of his missionary journeys. Paul gives Titus instructions about organizing the church and about the daily life of a Christian living in faith, emphasizing that godly living is always motivated by God's love for us in Christ Jesus.

Philemon: Paul writes this personal letter to Philemon, who is a slave owner. Paul intercedes for the runaway slave Onesimus, offering to pay off his debts and pleading that Philemon welcome him back. This is a picture of us as sinners who are slaves to sin. Jesus has paid the debt for our guilt and intercedes on our behalf before God the Father, who now welcomes us back to His family.

Hebrews: The remaining epistles are known as the General Epistles. The writer (unknown) to the Hebrews writes to Jewish communities, sharing information on the priesthood, with which they would be very familiar, to teach about the person and work of Jesus. It shows that Jesus is the fulfillment of the Old Testament laws and that He is greater than the prophets. Not only is He the great High Priest, He is also the perfect and complete sacrifice.

James: James is a practical book of Christian living. He wants people to understand that works are an important indication of faith and that "faith without works" is dead. Good works do not create saving faith, but when saving faith in Jesus exists, it is always followed with Christian living. (Justification is followed by sanctification.)

1 and 2 Peter: Peter writes these letters to people who are being persecuted for their faith. He reminds them that Jesus understands, for He suffered too. Jesus gives them an example of how to suffer and offers grace and hope in their time of trial. Peter reminds them that the troubles they face as Christians will make their faith strong. Peter warns about false teachers and encourages the people to be faithful until Christ comes again.

1, 2, and 3 John: John was an old man when he wrote these letters and often refers to the readers as his "dear children." He summarizes the love and mercy we have in Christ Jesus, which is our motivation to show love and mercy to others. John emphasizes that Jesus is both Son of God and Son of Man.

Jude: Jude (probably a half brother of Jesus) was written to Christians who have problems with false teachers. He reminds Christians that they are kept in their faith by Jesus. Jude challenges Christians of all times and all ages to stand up for what they believe in Christ and clearly protect the true faith.

Revelation: This book of prophecy is different from the other Bible books because it contains messages about the end of the world written in picture language. Revelation is a message from the apostle John, revealing, or showing, that Jesus will return triumphantly at His second coming. As Genesis starts with the beginning of time, Revelation speaks of the end of time, when we will see Jesus Christ's complete victory over sin, death, and the power of the devil. Christians are challenged to be strong and alive in their proclamation of faith and to remain faithful to the Last Day.

GRADE 5 CHRONOLOGY

Story of creation (Genesis 1)

Creation of Adam and Eve (Genesis 2)

The fall into sin (Genesis 3)

Faithful Enoch (Genesis 5:24)

Noah (Genesis 6:1–9:17; 1 Peter 3:18–22)

Sacrifice of Isaac (Genesis 22:1–18)

Joseph—a leader in Egypt (Genesis 41)

Old Testament Passover celebration (Exodus 12)

Deliverance at the Red Sea (Exodus 14–15)

Wilderness wanderings (Exodus 16:1–17:7)

God gives the Ten Commandments (Exodus 20)

Tabernacle gifts (Exodus 35:30–36:7)

Old Testament festivals (Leviticus 1–5)

The bronze serpent (Numbers 21:4–9)

Joshua's final message (Joshua 23:14; 24:14–15)

Gideon's call (Judges 6:1–24)

Gideon and the Midianites (Judges 7)

Ruth (Ruth)

Birth of Samuel (1 Samuel 1)

The call of Samuel (1 Samuel 3)

Saul's sacrifice (1 Samuel 13)

Young David (*shepherd, anointed, court musician*) (1 Samuel 16)

Psalms 19, 23, 51, 103, 150

Jonathan defends and warns David (1 Samuel 20)

David refuses to harm King Saul (1 Samuel 24; 26)

Abigail (1 Samuel 25:1–39)

David's prayer (2 Samuel 7:18–29)

Mephibosheth (2 Samuel 9)

David and Bathsheba (2 Samuel 11–12)

Absalom (2 Samuel 15; 18)

Solomon (1 Kings 3; 11:1-13)

Elijah and the Baal prophets (1 Kings 18:16–46)

Elijah in the cave (1 Kings 19:1–18)

Jehoshaphat (2 Chronicles 20:1–30)

Unfaithful Joash (2 Chronicles 24)

Jonah (Jonah 3)

Hezekiah (2 Kings 19)

Josiah (2 Chronicles 34)

Jeremiah's persistence (Jeremiah 5)

Daniel and the lions (Daniel 6)

Zechariah and the angel (Luke 1:5–25)

John the Baptist and his ministry (Luke 1:57–80; 3:1–18)

Birth of Jesus (Luke 2:1–20)

The presentation of baby Jesus (Luke 2:21; Matthew 1:21–23)

Simeon and Anna (Luke 2:22–40)

Boy Jesus in the temple (Luke 2:41–51)

Baptism of Jesus (Matthew 3:13–17)

Temptation of Jesus (Matthew 4:1–11)

John, Andrew, Peter meet Jesus (John 1:35–49)

Jesus calls His disciples (Luke 5 and 6)

Wedding of Cana (John 2:1–11)

Visit of Nicodemus (John 3:1–21)

Jesus walks away at Nazareth (Luke 4:14–30)

Jesus heals a paralyzed man (Mark 2:1–12)

Jesus and the centurion (Luke 7:1–10)

Jesus stills the storm (Mark 4:35–41)

Disciples ask Jesus about prayer (Matthew 6:1–14)

Parable of the sower (Matthew 13:1–23)

Jesus walks on water (Matthew 14:22–33)

Parable of two sons (Matthew 21:28–32)

Mary and Martha (Luke 10:38–42)

Parable of the lost sheep (Luke 15:1–7)

Parable of the prodigal son (Luke 15:11–24)

Lazarus's death (John 11:17–44)

Parable of the Pharisee and the tax collector (Luke 18:9–14)

The rich young man (Matthew 19:16–26)

Zacchaeus (Luke 19:1–10)

Palm Sunday in the temple (Matthew 21:12-17)

Widow's mite (Luke 21:1–4)

Maundy Thursday (Luke 22:7–23)

Jesus washes the disciples' feet (John 13:1–17)

Disciples argue about who is the greatest (Matthew 18:1–9; 19:13–15; 20:17–28; John 13:12–17)

Jesus in Gethsemane (Matthew 26:36–46)

The crucifixion (Luke 23:32–46)

Emmaus disciples at Easter (Luke 24:13–48)

Ascension (Acts 1:6–11; John 14:1–7)

Pentecost (Acts 2:1–18, 29–41)

Post-Pentecost Church (Acts 2:42–47)

Seven deacons chosen (Acts 6:1–7)

Peter before the council (Acts 4:1–20, 33)

Philip and the man from Africa (Acts 8:26–40)

Peter and Cornelius (Acts 10)

Peter is jailed (Acts 12)

Lydia (Acts 16:11–15)

Jailor at Philippi (Acts 16:16–34)

Paul at Mars Hill (Acts 17:16–32)

Paul trains Timothy (2 Timothy 1:3–10; 3:14–17)

Agrippa (Acts 25–26)

The Armor of God (Ephesians 6)

The Book of Colossians (Colossians)

Heaven and hell (Matthew 25:31–46; Revelation 21:1–8)

BIBLE CONCORDANCE

Based on the ESV
(English Standard Version)

ABUNDANT

Genesis 41:49 And Joseph stored up grain in great **abundan**ce, like the sand of the sea, until he ceased to measure it, for it could not be measured.

Numbers 20:11 Moses lifted up his hand and struck the rock with his staff twice, and water came out **abundant**ly, and the congregation drank.

Psalm 51:1 Have mercy on me, O God, according to Your steadfast love; according to Your **abundant** mercy blot out my transgressions.

Psalm 147:5 Great is our Lord, and **abundant** in power; His understanding is beyond measure.

John 10:10 I came that they may have life and have it **abundant**ly.

Ephesians 3:20–21 Now to Him who is able to do far more **abundant**ly than all that we ask or think, according to the power at work within us, to Him be glory in the church and in Christ Jesus throughout all generations, forever and ever. Amen.

BAPTIZE

Matthew 28:19 Go therefore and make disciples of all nations, **baptiz**ing them in the name of the Father and of the Son and of the Holy Spirit.

Acts 2:38 And Peter said to them, "Repent and be **baptize**d every one of you in the name of Jesus Christ for the forgiveness of your sins, and you will receive the gift of the Holy Spirit."

Galatians 3:27 For as many of you as were **baptize**d into Christ have put on Christ.

BELIEVE

John 6:40 For this is the will of My Father, that everyone who looks on the Son and **believe**s in Him should have eternal life, and I will raise him up on the last day.

John 11:25 Jesus said to her, "I am the resurrection and the life. Whoever **believe**s in Me, though he die, yet shall he live."

John 20:31 These are written so that you may **believe** that Jesus is the Christ, the Son of God, and that by **believ**ing you may have life in His name.

Acts 16:31 And they said, "**Believe** in the Lord Jesus, and you will be saved."

BENEFITS

Psalm 103:2 Bless the LORD, O my soul, and forget not all His **benefits**.

Psalm 116:12 What shall I render to the LORD for all His **benefits** to me?

CLEAN

Psalm 51:2 Wash me thoroughly from my iniquity, and **clean**se me from my sin!

Psalm 51:10 Create in me a **clean** heart, O God, and renew a right spirit within me.

1 John 1:9 If we confess our sins, He is faithful and just to forgive us our sins and to **clean**se us from all unrighteousness.

COMFORT

Psalm 23:4 Even though I walk through the valley of the shadow of death, I will fear no evil, for You are with me; Your rod and Your staff, they **comfort** me.

Psalm 119:50 This is my **comfort** in my affliction, that Your promise gives me life.

2 Corinthians 1:3 Blessed be the God and Father of our Lord Jesus Christ, the Father of mercies and God of all **comfort**.

2 Thessalonians 2:16–17 Now may our Lord Jesus Christ Himself, and God our Father, who loved us and gave us eternal **comfort** and good hope through grace, **comfort** your hearts and establish them in every good work and word.

COMPASSION

Isaiah 49:13 Sing for joy, O heavens, and exult, O earth; break forth, O mountains, into singing! For the LORD has comforted his people and will have **compassion** on his afflicted.

Colossians 3:12 Put on then, as God's chosen ones, holy and beloved, **compassion**ate hearts, kindness, humility, meekness, and patience.

CONFESS

Psalm 32:5 I acknowledged my sin to You, and I did not cover my iniquity; I said, "I will **confess** my transgressions to the LORD," and You forgave the iniquity of my sin.

Psalm 38:18 I **confess** my iniquity; I am sorry for my sin.

Romans 10:9 Because, if you **confess** with your mouth that Jesus is Lord and believe in your heart that God raised Him from the dead, you will be saved.

Philippians 2:11 And every tongue **confess** that Jesus Christ is Lord, to the glory of God the Father.

1 John 4:15 Whoever **confess**es that Jesus is the Son of God, God abides in him, and he in God.

CONTINUE

Acts 4:31 And when they had prayed, the place in which they were gathered together was shaken, and they were all filled with the Holy Spirit and **continue**d to speak the word of God with boldness.

Acts 13:43 And after the meeting of the synagogue broke up, many Jews and devout converts to Judaism followed Paul and Barnabas, who, as they spoke with them, urged them to **continue** in the grace of God.

Colossians 1:23 Continue in the faith, stable and steadfast, not shifting from the hope of the gospel that you heard, which has been proclaimed in all creation under heaven.

Colossians 4:2 Continue steadfastly in prayer, being watchful in it with thanksgiving.

2 Timothy 3:14 But as for you, **continue** in what you have learned and have firmly believed.

Hebrews 13:1 Let brotherly love **continue**.

COURAGE

Deuteronomy 31:6 Be strong and **courage**ous. Do not fear or be in dread of them, for it is the LORD your God who goes with you. He will not leave you or forsake you.

Joshua 1:9 Be strong and **courage**ous. Do not be frightened, and do not be dismayed, for the LORD your God is with you wherever you go.

Psalm 27:14 Wait for the Lord; be strong, and let your heart take **courage**; wait for the LORD!

CREATE

Psalm 51:10 Create in me a clean heart, O God, and renew a right spirit within me.

Isaiah 42:5 Thus says God, the LORD, who **create**d the heavens and stretched them out, who spread out the earth and what comes from it, who gives breath to the people on it and spirit to those who walk in it.

Ephesians 2:10 For we are His workmanship, **create**d in Christ Jesus for good works, which God prepared beforehand, that we should walk in them.

Ephesians 4:24 And to put on the new self, **create**d after the likeness of God in true righteousness and holiness.

Colossians 1:16 For by Him all things were **create**d, in heaven and on earth, visible and invisible, whether thrones or dominions or rulers or authorities—all things were **create**d through Him and for Him.

Hebrews 1:2 But in these last days He has spoken to us by His Son, whom He appointed the heir of all things, through whom also He **create**d the world.

Revelation 4:11 Worthy are You, our Lord and God, to receive glory and honor and power, for You **create**d all things, and by Your will they existed and were **create**d.

CREATION

Mark 16:15 And He said to them, "Go into all the world and proclaim the gospel to the whole **creation**."

2 Corinthians 5:17 Therefore, if anyone is in Christ, he is a new **creation**. The old has passed away; behold, the new has come.

ENCOURAGE

Romans 15:4 For whatever was written in former days was written for our instruction, that through endurance and through the **encourage**ment of the Scriptures we might have hope.

Romans 15:5 May the God of endurance and **encourage**ment grant you to live in such harmony with one another, in accord with Christ Jesus.

1 Thessalonians 5:11 Therefore **encourage** one another and build one another up, just as you are doing.

ENDURE

Psalm 100:5 For the Lord is good; His steadfast love **endure**s forever, and His faithfulness to all generations.

Psalm 104:31 May the glory of the Lord **endure** forever; may the Lord rejoice in His works.

Psalm 117:2 For great is His steadfast love toward us, and the faithfulness of the Lord **endure**s forever. Praise the Lord!

Psalm 135:13 Your name, O Lord, **endure**s forever, Your renown, O Lord, throughout all ages.

Psalm 136:1 Give thanks to the Lord, for He is good, for his steadfast love **endure**s forever.

Lamentations 5:19 But You, O Lord, reign forever; Your throne **endure**s to all generations.

Hebrews 12:2 Looking to Jesus, the founder and perfecter of our faith, who for the joy that was set before Him **endure**d the cross, despising the shame, and is seated at the right hand of the throne of God.

ETERNAL

John 3:16 For God so loved the world, that He gave His only Son, that whoever believes in Him should not perish but have **eternal** life.

John 6:40 For this is the will of My Father, that everyone who looks on the Son and believes in Him should have **eternal** life, and I will raise him up on the last day.

Titus 3:7 So that being justified by His grace we might become heirs according to the hope of **eternal** life.

FAITH

Galatians 3:11 Now it is evident that no one is justified before God by the law, for "The righteous shall live by **faith**."

Ephesians 2:8 For by grace you have been saved through **faith**. And this is not your own doing; it is the gift of God.

1 Timothy 1:14 And the grace of our Lord overflowed for me with the **faith** and love that are in Christ Jesus.

1 Timothy 4:12 Let no one despise you for your youth, but set the believers an example in speech, in conduct, in love, in **faith**, in purity.

FAITHFUL

Psalm 86:15 But You, O Lord, are a God merciful and gracious, slow to anger and abounding in steadfast love and **faithful**ness.

1 John 1:9 If we confess our sins, He is **faithful** and just to forgive us our sins and to cleanse us from all unrighteousness.

Revelation 2:10 Be **faithful** unto death, and I will give you the crown of life.

FORGIVE

Ephesians 1:7 In Him we have redemption through His blood, the **forgive**ness of our trespasses, according to the riches of His grace.

Colossians 3:13 Bearing with one another and, if one has a complaint against another, forgiving each other; as the Lord has **forgive**n you, so you also must **forgive**.

GRACE

Romans 1:7 To all those in Rome who are loved by God and called to be saints: **Grace** to you and peace from God our Father and the Lord Jesus Christ.

Romans 3:24 And are justified by His **grace** as a gift, through the redemption that is in Christ Jesus.

2 Corinthians 9:8 And God is able to make all **grace** abound to you, so that having all sufficiency in all things at all times, you may abound in every good work.

Ephesians 2:8 For by **grace** you have been saved through faith. And this is not your own doing; it is the gift of God.

2 Peter 3:18 But grow in the **grace** and knowledge of our Lord and Savior Jesus Christ. To Him be the glory both now and to the day of eternity. Amen.

HELP

Psalm 18:6 In my distress I called upon the LORD; to my God I cried for **help**. From His temple He heard my voice, and my cry to Him reached His ears.

Psalm 28:7 The LORD is my strength and my shield; in Him my heart trusts, and I am **help**ed; my heart exults, and with my song I give thanks to Him.

Psalm 40:13 Be pleased, O LORD, to deliver me! O LORD, make haste to **help** me!

Psalm 79:9 **Help** us, O God of our salvation, for the glory of Your name; deliver us, and atone for our sins, for Your name's sake!

Psalm 124:8 Our **help** is in the name of the LORD, who made heaven and earth.

John 14:26 But the **Help**er, the Holy Spirit, whom the Father will send in My name, He will teach you all things and bring to your remembrance all that I have said to you.

Acts 26:22 To this day I have had the **help** that comes from God.

Romans 8:26 Likewise the Spirit **help**s us in our weakness. For we do not know what to pray for as we ought, but the Spirit Himself intercedes for us with groanings too deep for words.

Hebrews 4:16 Let us then with confidence draw near to the throne of grace, that we may receive mercy and find grace to **help** in time of need.

Hebrews 13:6 So we can confidently say, "The Lord is my **help**er; I will not fear; what can man do to me?"

HOLY

Psalm 97:12 Rejoice in the LORD, O you righteous, and give thanks to His **holy** name!

Psalm 103:1 Bless the LORD, O my soul, and all that is within me, bless His **holy** name!

Isaiah 6:3 And one called to another and said: "**Holy, holy, holy** is the LORD of hosts; the whole earth is full of His glory!"

Acts 2:38 And Peter said to them, "Repent and be baptized every one of you in the name of Jesus Christ for the forgiveness of your sins, and you will receive the gift of the **Holy** Spirit."

Romans 15:13 May the God of hope fill you with all joy and peace in believing, so that by the power of the **Holy** Spirit you may abound in hope.

HOPE

Psalm 33:22 Let Your steadfast love, O LORD, be upon us, even as we **hope** in You.

Psalm 42:11 Why are you cast down, O my soul, and why are you in turmoil within me? **Hope** in God; for I shall again praise Him, my salvation and my God.

Psalm 71:5 For You, O Lord, are my **hope**, my trust, O LORD, from my youth.

Psalm 119:114 You are my hiding place and my shield; I **hope** in Your word.

Psalm 147:11 But the LORD takes pleasure in those who fear Him, in those who **hope** in His steadfast love.

Hebrews 10:23 Let us hold fast the confession of our **hope** without wavering, for He who promised is faithful.

Hebrews 11:1 Now faith is the assurance of things **hope**d for, the conviction of things not seen.

1 Peter 1:3 Blessed be the God and Father of our Lord Jesus Christ! According to His great mercy, He has caused us to be born again to a living **hope** through the resurrection of Jesus Christ from the dead.

1 Peter 3:15 But in your hearts honor Christ the Lord as holy, always being prepared to make a defense to anyone who asks you for a reason for the **hope** that is in you; yet do it with gentleness and respect.

Colossians 1:23 Continue in the faith, stable and steadfast, not shifting from the **hope** of the gospel that you heard, which has been proclaimed in all creation under heaven.

Titus 3:7 So that being justified by His grace we might become heirs according to the **hope** of eternal life.

JUSTIFY

Romans 3:24 And [we] are **justif**ied by His grace as a gift, through the redemption that is in Christ Jesus.

Romans 5:1 Therefore, since we have been **justif**ied by faith, we have peace with God through our Lord Jesus Christ.

Galatians 3:11 Now it is evident that no one is **justif**ied before God by the law, for "The righteous shall live by faith."

LAMB

John 1:29 The next day he saw Jesus coming toward him, and said, "Behold, the **Lamb** of God, who takes away the sin of the world!"

Revelation 5:12 Saying with a loud voice, "Worthy is the **Lamb** who was slain, to receive power and wealth and wisdom and might and honor and glory and blessing!"

LIGHT

Psalm 27:1 The LORD is my **light** and my salvation; whom shall I fear? The LORD is the stronghold of my life; of whom shall I be afraid?

Psalm 119:105 Your word is a lamp to my feet and a **light** to my path.

John 8:12 Again Jesus spoke to them, saying, "I am the **light** of the world. Whoever follows Me will not walk in darkness, but will have the **light** of life."

1 John 1:7 But if we walk in the **light**, as He is in the **light**, we have fellowship with one another, and the blood of Jesus His Son cleanses us from all sin.

MERCY

Psalm 23:6 Surely goodness and **mercy** shall follow me all the days of my life, and I shall dwell in the house of the LORD forever.

Psalm 145:9 The LORD is good to all, and His **mercy** is over all that He has made.

Hebrews 4:16 Let us then with confidence draw near to the throne of grace, that we may receive **mercy** and find grace to help in time of need.

PEACE

Isaiah 9:6 For to us a child is born, to us a son is given; and the government shall be upon His shoulder, and His name shall be called Wonderful Counselor, Mighty God, Everlasting Father, Prince of **Peace**.

Luke 2:14 Glory to God in the highest, and on earth **peace**.

John 14:27 **Peace** I leave with you; My **peace** I give to you. Not as the world gives do I give to you. Let not your hearts be troubled, neither let them be afraid.

Romans 5:1 Therefore, since we have been justified by faith, we have **peace** with God through our Lord Jesus Christ.

Philippians 4:7 And the **peace** of God, which surpasses all understanding, will guard your hearts and your minds in Christ Jesus.

PERSECUTION

Matthew 5:10 Blessed are those who are **persecut**ed for righteousness' sake, for theirs is the kingdom of heaven.

Matthew 5:11 Blessed are you when others revile you and **persecut**e you and utter all kinds of evil against you falsely on My account.

Matthew 5:44 But I say to you, Love your enemies and pray for those who **persecut**e you.

1 Corinthians 4:12 And we labor, working with our own hands. When reviled, we bless; when **persecut**ed, we endure.

REDEEM/REDEMPTION

Job 19:25 For I know that my **Redeem**er lives, and at the last he will stand upon the earth.

Isaiah 43:1 But now thus says the LORD, He who created you, . . . "Fear not, for I have **redeem**ed you; I have called you by name, you are Mine."

Ephesians 1:7 In Him we have **redemption** through His blood, the forgiveness of our trespasses, according to the riches of His grace.

RENEW

Psalm 51:10 Create in me a clean heart, O God, and **renew** a right spirit within me.

Isaiah 40:31 But they who wait for the LORD shall **renew** their strength; they shall mount up with wings like eagles; they shall run and not be weary; they shall walk and not faint.

Romans 12:2 Do not be conformed to this world, but be transformed by the **renew**al of your mind, that by testing you may discern what is the will of God, what is good and acceptable and perfect.

Titus 3:5 He saved us, not because of works done by us in righteousness, but according to His own mercy, by the washing of regeneration and **renew**al of the Holy Spirit.

RESURRECTION

John 11:25 Jesus said to her, "I am the **resurrection** and the life. Whoever believes in Me, though he die, yet shall he live."

Romans 6:5 For if we have been united with Him in a death like His, we shall certainly be united with Him in a **resurrection** like His.

1 Peter 1:3 Blessed be the God and Father of our Lord Jesus Christ! According to His great mercy, He has caused us to be born again to a living hope through the **resurrection** of Jesus Christ from the dead.

SAVE

Acts 4:12 And there is salvation in no one else, for there is no other name under heaven given among men by which we must be **saved**.

1 Timothy 1:15 The saying is trustworthy and deserving of full acceptance, that Christ Jesus came into the world to **save** sinners, of whom I am the foremost.

SEPARATE

Romans 8:35 Who shall **separate** us from the love of Christ? Shall tribulation, or distress, or persecution, or famine, or nakedness, or danger, or sword?

Romans 8:38–39 I am sure that neither death nor life, nor angels nor rulers, nor things present nor things to come, nor powers, nor height nor depth, nor anything else in all creation, will be able to **separate** us from the love of God in Christ Jesus our Lord.

SERVE

Psalm 100:2 Serve the LORD with gladness! Come into His presence with singing!

Mark 10:45 For even the Son of Man came not to be **serve**d but to **serve**, and to give His life as a ransom for many.

SHEEP

Psalm 95:7 For He is our God, and we are the people of His pasture, and the **sheep** of His hand.

Psalm 100:3 Know that the LORD, He is God! It is He who made us, and we are His; we are His people, and the **sheep** of His pasture.

Isaiah 53:6 All we like **sheep** have gone astray; we have turned—every one—to his own way; and the LORD has laid on him the iniquity of us all.

Ezekiel 34:15 I Myself will be the shepherd of my **sheep**, and I Myself will make them lie down, declares the Lord GOD.

John 10:11 I am the good shepherd. The good shepherd lays down His life for the **sheep**.

John 10:27 My **sheep** hear My voice, and I know them, and they follow Me.

SHEPHERD

Psalm 23:1 The LORD is my **shepherd**; I shall not want.

Isaiah 40:11 He will tend His flock like a **shepherd**; He will gather the lambs in His arms; He will carry them in His bosom, and gently lead those that are with young.

John 10:11 I am the good **shepherd**. The good **shepherd** lays down His life for the sheep.

John 10:14 I am the good **shepherd**. I know My own and My own know Me.

SIN

Psalm 32:5 I acknowledged my **sin** to you, and I did not cover my iniquity; I said, "I will confess my transgressions to the LORD," and You forgave the iniquity of my **sin**.

Psalm 38:18 I confess my iniquity; I am sorry for my **sin**.

Psalm 41:4 As for me, I said, "O LORD, be gracious to me; heal me, for I have **sin**ned against You!"

Psalm 51:2 Wash me thoroughly from my iniquity, and cleanse me from my **sin**.

Romans 3:23 For all have **sin**ned and fall short of the glory of God.

Romans 5:8 But God shows His love for us in that while we were still **sin**ners, Christ died for us.

Romans 6:23 For the wages of **sin** is death, but the free gift of God is eternal life in Christ Jesus our Lord.

1 Corinthians 15:3 For I delivered to you as of first importance what I also received: that Christ died for our **sin**s in accordance with the Scriptures.

2 Corinthians 5:21 For our sake He made Him to be **sin** who knew no **sin**, so that in Him we might become the righteousness of God.

SING

Psalm 30:4 Sing praises to the LORD, O you His saints, and give thanks to His holy name.

Psalm 57:9 I will give thanks to You, O Lord, among the peoples; I will **sing** praises to You among the nations.

Psalm 89:1 I will **sing** of the steadfast love of the LORD, forever; with my mouth I will make known Your faithfulness to all generations.

Psalm 95:1 Oh come, let us **sing** to the LORD; let us make a joyful noise to the rock of our salvation!

Psalm 96:1 Oh **sing** to the LORD a new song; **sing** to the LORD, all the earth!

Psalm 96:2 Sing to the LORD, bless His name; tell of His salvation from day to day.

Psalm 146:2 I will praise the LORD as long as I live; I will **sing** praises to my God while I have my being.

SPIRIT

Acts 1:8 "But you will receive power when the Holy **Spirit** has come upon you, and you will be my witnesses in Jerusalem and in all Judea and Samaria, and to the end of the earth."

Acts 2:4 And they were all filled with the Holy **Spirit** and began to speak in other tongues as the **Spirit** gave them utterance.

Acts 4:31 And when they had prayed, the place in which they were gathered together was shaken, and they were all filled with the Holy **Spirit** and continued to speak the word of God with boldness.

Acts 9:17 So Ananias departed and entered the house. And laying his hands on him he said, "Brother Saul, the Lord Jesus who appeared to you on the road by which you came has sent me so that you may regain your sight and be filled with the Holy **Spirit**."

Acts 13:52 And the disciples were filled with joy and with the Holy **Spirit**.

Acts 19:5-6 On hearing this, they were baptized in the name of the Lord Jesus. And when Paul had laid his hands on them, the Holy **Spirit** came on them.

Strength

Psalm 28:7 The LORD is my **strength** and my shield; in Him my heart trusts, and I am helped; my heart exults, and with my song I give thanks to Him.

Psalm 29:11 May the LORD give **strength** to His people! May the LORD bless His people with peace!

Psalm 73:26 My flesh and my heart may fail, but God is the **strength** of my heart and my portion forever.

Psalm 96:7 Ascribe to the LORD, O families of the peoples, ascribe to the LORD glory and **strength**!

Psalm 118:14 The LORD is my **strength** and my song; He has become my salvation.

Ephesians 6:10 Finally, be strong in the Lord and in the **strength** of His might.

Philippians 4:13 I can do all things through Him who **strength**ens me.

TEMPLE

2 Chronicles 7:1 As soon as Solomon finished his prayer, fire came down from heaven and consumed the burnt offering and the sacrifices, and the glory of the LORD filled the **temple**.

2 Chronicles 7:3 When all the people of Israel saw the fire come down and the glory of the LORD on the **temple**, they bowed down with their faces to the ground on the pavement and worshiped and gave thanks to the LORD, saying, "For He is good, for His steadfast love endures forever."

Habakkuk 2:20 But the LORD is in His holy **temple**; let all the earth keep silence before Him.

Luke 2:46 After three days they found Him in the **temple**, sitting among the teachers, listening to them and asking them questions.

John 2:19 Jesus answered them, "Destroy this **temple**, and in three days I will raise it up."

John 2:21 But He was speaking about the **temple** of His body.

Acts 5:42 And every day, in the **temple** and from house to house, they did not cease teaching and preaching Jesus as the Christ.

Acts 17:24 The God who made the world and everything in it, being Lord of heaven and earth, does not live in **temple**s made by man.

1 Corinthians 3:16 Do you not know that you are God's **temple** and that God's Spirit dwells in you?

1 Corinthians 6:19 Or do you not know that your body is a **temple** of the Holy Spirit within you, whom you have from God? You are not your own.

WORSHIP

Psalm 29:2 Ascribe to the LORD the glory due His name; **worship** the LORD in the splendor of holiness.

Psalm 86:9 All the nations you have made shall come and **worship** before you, O Lord, and shall glorify Your name.

Psalm 95:6 Oh come, let us **worship** and bow down; let us kneel before the LORD, our Maker!

Luke 4:8 And Jesus answered him, "It is written, 'You shall **worship** the Lord your God, and Him only shall you serve.'"

John 4:24 God is spirit, and those who **worship** Him must **worship** in spirit and truth.

Romans 12:1 I appeal to you therefore, brothers, by the mercies of God, to present your bodies as a living sacrifice, holy and acceptable to God, which is your spiritual **worship**.

Old Testament
CHRONOLOGY

Creation
Fall
Flood
Babel
Genesis 1–11

LINES TO TIME LINE DENOTE
END OF
JOURNEY OR REIGN

LINES DENOTE LAST YEAR OF
REIGN OR LIFE,
CO-REGENCIES AND SHORT
REIGNS OMITTED.

(2300 B.C. – 1700 B.C.)

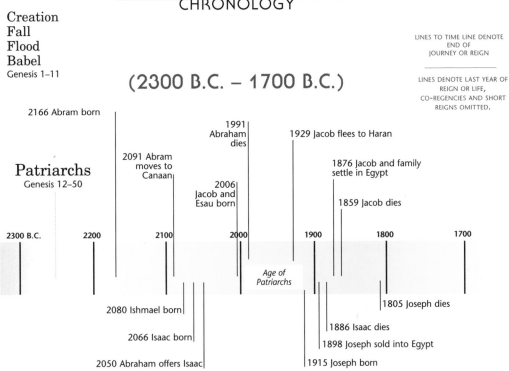

2166 Abram born

Patriarchs
Genesis 12–50

2091 Abram moves to Canaan

1991 Abraham dies

1929 Jacob flees to Haran

1876 Jacob and family settle in Egypt

2006 Jacob and Esau born

1859 Jacob dies

2300 B.C.   2200   2100   2000   1900   1800   1700

Age of Patriarchs

2080 Ishmael born

1805 Joseph dies

2066 Isaac born

1886 Isaac dies

2050 Abraham offers Isaac

1898 Joseph sold into Egypt

1915 Joseph born

(1600 B.C. – 900 B.C.)

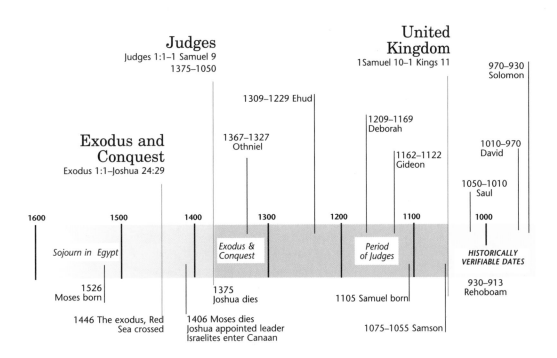

Judges
Judges 1:1–1 Samuel 9
1375–1050

United Kingdom
1Samuel 10–1 Kings 11

970–930 Solomon

1309–1229 Ehud

1209–1169 Deborah

Exodus and Conquest
Exodus 1:1–Joshua 24:29

1367–1327 Othniel

1162–1122 Gideon

1010–970 David

1050–1010 Saul

1600   1500   1400   1300   1200   1100   1000

Sojourn in Egypt

Exodus & Conquest

Period of Judges

HISTORICALLY VERIFIABLE DATES

1526 Moses born

1375 Joshua dies

1105 Samuel born

930–913 Rehoboam

1446 The exodus, Red Sea crossed

1406 Moses dies
Joshua appointed leader
Israelites enter Canaan

1075–1055 Samson

Old Testament
CHRONOLOGY

(900 B.C. – 400 B.C.)

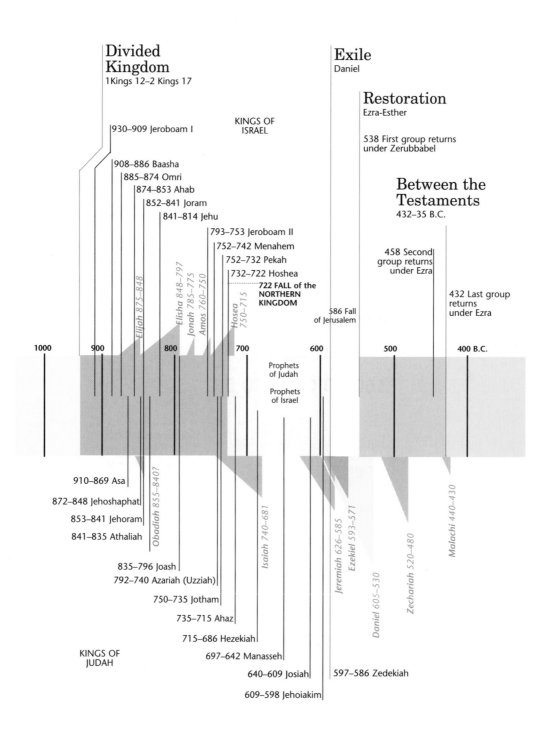

**Divided
Kingdom**
1Kings 12–2 Kings 17

Exile
Daniel

Restoration
Ezra-Esther

538 First group returns
under Zerubbabel

KINGS OF
ISRAEL

930–909 Jeroboam I

908–886 Baasha
885–874 Omri
874–853 Ahab
852–841 Joram
841–814 Jehu

793–753 Jeroboam II
752–742 Menahem
752–732 Pekah
732–722 Hoshea
**722 FALL of the
NORTHERN
KINGDOM**

**Between the
Testaments**
432–35 B.C.

458 Second
group returns
under Ezra

432 Last group
returns
under Ezra

586 Fall
of Jerusalem

Elijah 875–848

Elisha 848–797
Jonah 785–775
Amos 760–750

*Hosea
750–715*

1000   900   800   700   600   500   400 B.C.

Prophets
of Judah

Prophets
of Israel

910–869 Asa

872–848 Jehoshaphat

853–841 Jehoram

841–835 Athaliah

Obadiah 855–840?

835–796 Joash
792–740 Azariah (Uzziah)

750–735 Jotham

735–715 Ahaz

715–686 Hezekiah

697–642 Manasseh

640–609 Josiah

609–598 Jehoiakim

Isaiah 740–681

Jeremiah 626–585
Ezekiel 593–571

Daniel 605–530

Zechariah 520–480

Malachi 440–430

597–586 Zedekiah

KINGS OF
JUDAH

New Testament
CHRONOLOGY

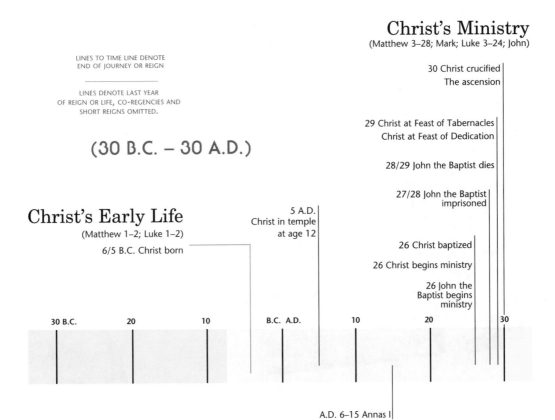

Christ's Ministry
(Matthew 3–28; Mark; Luke 3–24; John)

LINES TO TIME LINE DENOTE
END OF JOURNEY OR REIGN

LINES DENOTE LAST YEAR
OF REIGN OR LIFE, CO-REGENCIES AND
SHORT REIGNS OMITTED.

(30 B.C. – 30 A.D.)

30 Christ crucified
The ascension

29 Christ at Feast of Tabernacles
Christ at Feast of Dedication

28/29 John the Baptist dies

27/28 John the Baptist
imprisoned

Christ's Early Life
(Matthew 1–2; Luke 1–2)

5 A.D.
Christ in temple
at age 12

6/5 B.C. Christ born

26 Christ baptized

26 Christ begins ministry

26 John the
Baptist begins
ministry

30 B.C.   20   10   B.C. A.D.   10   20   30

A.D. 6–15 Annas I

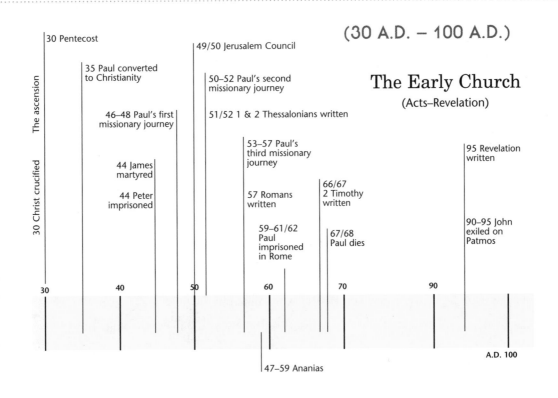

(30 A.D. – 100 A.D.)

30 Pentecost

49/50 Jerusalem Council

35 Paul converted
to Christianity

50–52 Paul's second
missionary journey

The Early Church
(Acts–Revelation)

The ascension

46–48 Paul's first
missionary journey

51/52 1 & 2 Thessalonians written

53–57 Paul's
third missionary
journey

95 Revelation
written

30 Christ crucified

44 James
martyred

44 Peter
imprisoned

57 Romans
written

66/67
2 Timothy
written

59–61/62
Paul
imprisoned
in Rome

67/68
Paul dies

90–95 John
exiled on
Patmos

30   40   50   60   70   90

A.D. 100

47–59 Ananias

TO THE PROMISED LAND

A view of the Great Sphinx with the Great Pyramid of Khufu in the background in Giza, Egypt.

© Ramzi Hachicho/Shutterstock, Inc.

The Great Sea
(Mediterranean Sea)

•Damascus

Yarmuk River

Jordan River

Jabbok River

CANAAN

Shechem

GILEAD

•Bethel

PHILISTIA

Mount
Moriah

•Ephrath

NEGEB

MOAB

▲Mount Seir

EDOM

ARABIA

Rosetta

Alexandria

Rameses

GOSHEN

•Pi-hahiroth

WILDERNESS
OF SHUR

EGYPT

•Cairo

Memphis •

SINAI

•Marah

Nile River

•Elim

WILDERNESS
OF SIN

MIDIAN

•Meribah

Gulf of Aqaba

•Rephidim

Gulf of Suez

Mount Sinai
(Horeb)

N

E

W

S

WILDERNESS
OF SINAI

•Karnak
•Luxor

Red Sea

PADDAN ARAM

Euphrates River

Tigris River

M E S O P O T A M I A

Euphrates River

Ur •

Mount Sinai, where God gave the
Ten Commandments to His people.

© George Muresan/Shutterstock, Inc.

© Kavram/Shutterstock, Inc.

The Sinai Desert.
The children of Israel
traveled through this
land on their way to
Canaan.

0

0

500 Miles

500 KM

The Divided Kingdom 900 BC

- Damascus
- Sidon
PHOENICIA
- Zarephath
▲ *Mt. Hermon*
- Dan
- Tyre
- Kedesh
- Hazor
- Janoah
- Ramah
ARAM
- Chinnereth
Sea of Galilee
Mt. Carmel ▲
- Jabneel
- Jokneam *Mt. Tabor* ▲
- Lo-debar
- Dor
- Shunem
- Megiddo
- Jezreel
- Tishbe?
- Taanach *Mt. Gilboa* ▲
- Jabesh-gilead
- Beth-haggan
Jordan R.
- Ibleam
- Gath
- Tirzah
- Zarethan
- Socoh
Cherith Ravine
- Penuel
- Samaria
- Adam
- Pirathon
- Shechem
AMMON
- Aphek
- Joppa
- Lod
- Bethel
- Gimzo
- Jericho
- Jerusalem
ISRAEL
- Bethlehem
- Lachish
- Adoraim
- Ziph
- Engedi
- Eshtemoa
- Carmel
- Maon
MOAB
- Arad
- Beersheba
- Hormah
- Aroer
PHILISTIA

JUDAH

EASTERN DESERT

EDOM

The Land Of Jesus

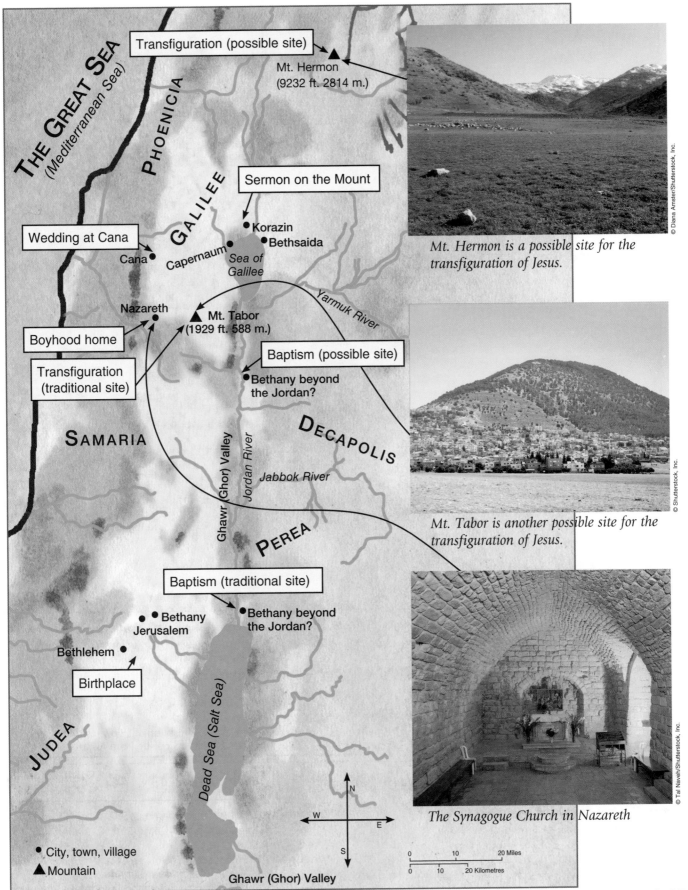

Transfiguration (possible site)

Mt. Hermon
(9232 ft. 2814 m.)

THE GREAT SEA
(Mediterranean Sea)

PHOENICIA

GALILEE

Sermon on the Mount

Korazin
Bethsaida

Wedding at Cana

Cana
Capernaum
Sea of Galilee

Yarmuk River

Nazareth
Mt. Tabor
(1929 ft. 588 m.)

Boyhood home

Baptism (possible site)

Transfiguration
(traditional site)

Bethany beyond
the Jordan?

SAMARIA

DECAPOLIS

Ghawr (Ghor) Valley
Jordan River

Jabbok River

PEREA

Baptism (traditional site)

Bethany
Jerusalem

Bethany beyond
the Jordan?

Bethlehem

Birthplace

Dead Sea (Salt Sea)

JUDEA

N
W   E
S

• City, town, village
▲ Mountain

Ghawr (Ghor) Valley

0   10   20 Miles
0   10   20 Kilometres

Mt. Hermon is a possible site for the transfiguration of Jesus.

© Diana Amster/Shutterstock, Inc.

Mt. Tabor is another possible site for the transfiguration of Jesus.

© Shutterstock, Inc.

The Synagogue Church in Nazareth

© Tal Naveh/Shutterstock, Inc.

Paul's Missionary Journeys

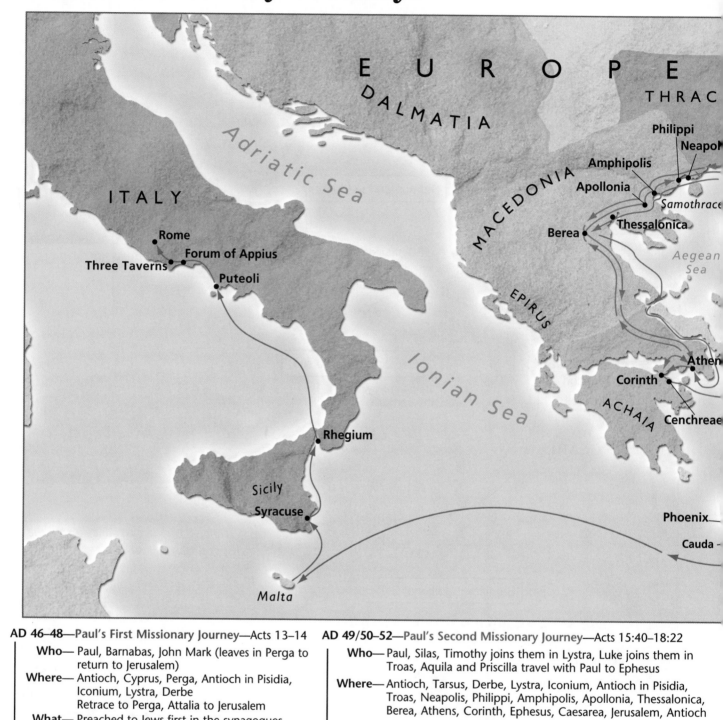

AD 46–48—Paul's First Missionary Journey—Acts 13–14

Who— Paul, Barnabas, John Mark (leaves in Perga to return to Jerusalem)

Where— Antioch, Cyprus, Perga, Antioch in Pisidia, Iconium, Lystra, Derbe
Retrace to Perga, Attalia to Jerusalem

What— Preached to Jews first in the synagogues, then to Gentiles

AD 49/50–52—Paul's Second Missionary Journey—Acts 15:40–18:22

Who— Paul, Silas, Timothy joins them in Lystra, Luke joins them in Troas, Aquila and Priscilla travel with Paul to Ephesus

Where— Antioch, Tarsus, Derbe, Lystra, Iconium, Antioch in Pisidia, Troas, Neapolis, Philippi, Amphipolis, Apollonia, Thessalonica, Berea, Athens, Corinth, Ephesus, Caesarea, Jerusalem, Antioch

What— Preached to Jews and Gentiles
Paul wrote 1 and 2 Thessalonians Epistles from Corinth
Paul wrote the Galatians Epistle from Antioch

250	BC✝AD		1		36	37	38	39	40	41	42	43	44	45	46	48	4

 First Missionary Journey (AD 46–48)

← Second Missionary Journey (AD 49/50–52)

← Third Missionary Journey (AD 52/53–57)

← Trip to Rome (AD 59–61/62)

AD 49/50—Jerusalem Council—Acts 15

Who— Paul, Barnabas, James, Peter, Silas

Where— Jerusalem

What— Met with leaders of the entire Church, who then wrote a letter to Gentile Christians in Antioch
Paul and Silas partner; Barnabas and John Mark partner

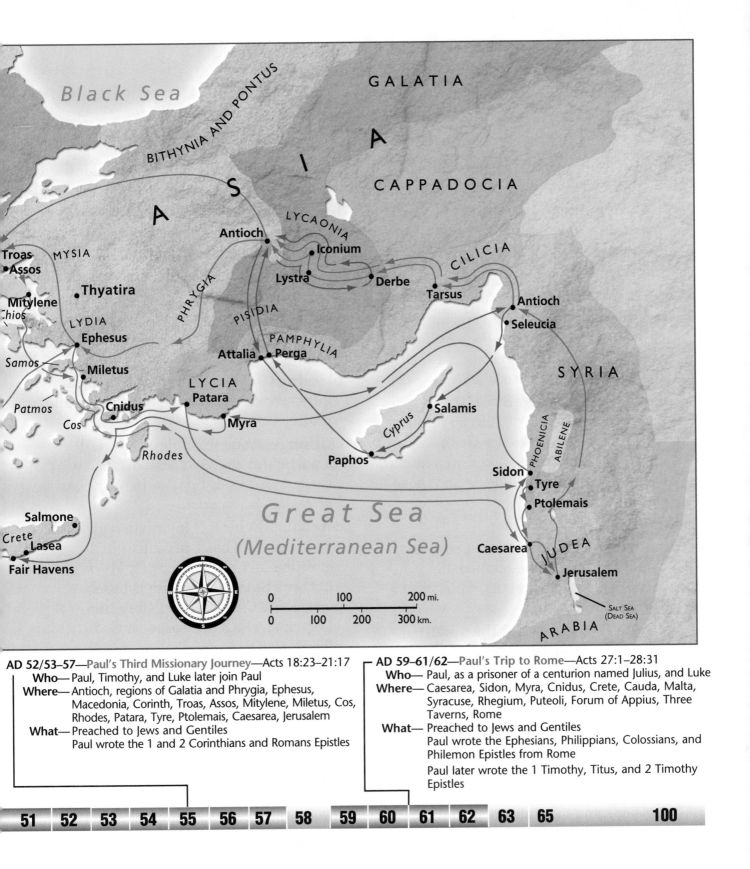

AD 52/53–57—Paul's Third Missionary Journey—Acts 18:23–21:17

Who— Paul, Timothy, and Luke later join Paul

Where— Antioch, regions of Galatia and Phrygia, Ephesus, Macedonia, Corinth, Troas, Assos, Mitylene, Miletus, Cos, Rhodes, Patara, Tyre, Ptolemais, Caesarea, Jerusalem

What— Preached to Jews and Gentiles
Paul wrote the 1 and 2 Corinthians and Romans Epistles

AD 59–61/62—Paul's Trip to Rome—Acts 27:1–28:31

Who— Paul, as a prisoner of a centurion named Julius, and Luke

Where— Caesarea, Sidon, Myra, Cnidus, Crete, Cauda, Malta, Syracuse, Rhegium, Puteoli, Forum of Appius, Three Taverns, Rome

What— Preached to Jews and Gentiles
Paul wrote the Ephesians, Philippians, Colossians, and Philemon Epistles from Rome

Paul later wrote the 1 Timothy, Titus, and 2 Timothy Epistles

51	52	53	54	55	56	57	58	59	60	61	62	63	65	100

Glossary

abortion Taking the life of an unborn person.

absolution An announcement or declaration of forgiveness.

abundance More than enough; more than we need.

advent Something or someone is coming.

almighty This adjective means having all power, unlimited might. *Body builders may be strong. Earthly rulers may be powerful. Only God is almighty.*

angel A spirit being, created by God, having a mind and will, but no physical body (though, at times, for God's purposes, angels have taken on a human form). There are good angels and those that turned evil.

atlas A collection of maps.

atonement The payment that pays the penalty to correct the relationship between God and humans, which was broken through sin.

attitude How you look at the world; perspective; viewpoint; point of view; mind-set; outlook; how you observe, understand, and perceive things. *Attitudes can be positive or negative. If you look for good, you will find it. If you expect problems, they will probably happen.*

authority Having power to make decisions and to establish and enforce commands and rules.

avoid To keep away from.

baptismal font Receptacle for water used in Baptism.

benediction Proclamation of a blessing, especially the short blessing with which public worship is concluded.

betray To tell someone's secrets; to act disloyally.

bless (1) To give joy or gifts. (2) To pray for someone's welfare. (3) To give God glory and praise.

blessing God blesses us with His good gifts; we bless Him with our thanks and praise.

calling A strong inner desire toward a particular course of action. *Often a person's calling is fulfilled in their chosen profession or vocation.*

catechism A book of instruction giving a summary of basic principles in a question-and-answer format. Martin Luther's Small Catechism is based on the Six Chief Parts of Christian Doctrine, which are based on God's Word.

chant To sing with repetitive tones.

charity (1) Kindness shown, especially to those in need. (2) Love. *In older translations of 1 Corinthians 13, the word love has been translated as charity.*

chaste Morally and sexually clean and pure.

cherubim Angels of a specific rank or grouping; in Hebrew, the word implies nearness, perhaps indicating the cherubim's nearness to God. These angels are sometimes described as having four wings.

Christ Greek for "Messiah."

Christian discipleship The actions of being a disciple—listening, supporting, and living in faith, following the ways and will of our Lord Jesus.

cling To hold on tightly, firmly, tenaciously.

collaborate To work jointly with others, especially in an intellectual endeavor.

commit (1) To put in charge or entrust. (2) To carry into action deliberately.

communicant Someone who is eligible to receive Holy Communion.

compassion Feeling the joy or the sadness of someone else, leading to a positive response.

condemnation Being judged and found guilty for your actions.

confession (1) Stating accurately what we believe is true. (2) Admitting sins and recognizing what God says about our wrongdoing.

consecrate To set someone or something apart for a special, holy purpose.

consequence The result of an action.

contrition Sincere regret or sorrow for one's sins; remorse.

conversion A change, turn around, transformation; new life in Christ.

cooperation Acting together toward a common purpose.

coordination Harmonious adjustments and interactions.

covenant A promise or pledge; a formal agreement. An agreement of faithfulness. "I will walk among you and will be your God, and you shall be My people" (Leviticus 26:12).

culture The socially shared behavior patterns, arts, beliefs, institutions that characterize an ethnic, religious, or social group (including shared attitudes, values, goals, and practices that characterize that particular group).

curse (1) To speak evil of God or mock Him. (2) To call God's anger down on someone or something.

decent Meeting accepted standards of moral behavior.

demons Evil angels; a name for the angels who joined Satan when he rebelled against God.

denomination A religious organization uniting congregations in a single administrative body.

despise Neglect, ignore.

Devil Another name for Satan; this name means "slanderer" or "accuser." Because of Jesus' death on the cross, our heavenly Father does not listen to Satan's accusations.

devote To set apart for a special person or for a special reason; to set apart for God's use.

disciple One who listens, understands, and follows the teachings and beliefs of another. See also *Christian discipleship*.

empower When an outside source gives you the power or ability to do or be something.

emulate Strive for accomplishments similar to someone else.

enable When an outside source helps you to be able to do something or makes it possible to be something.

enchiridion Refers to the brief portion of questions and answers written by Luther, which is often memorized by people who study Christian doctrine, which is based on God's Word. In the book *Luther's Small Catechism with Explanation,* the enchiridion is the first small section of the book (approximately 10 percent), followed by a deeper exploration of the enchiridion itself.

endure To last a long time; continue.

environment Surroundings, conditions, influences, external factors affecting us and our lives.

envy To want for oneself something that belongs to another person.

epistle A letter; often meaning the letters in the Bible written by an apostle.

esteem To think highly of someone or something; to respect.

euthanasia Ending the life of someone too infirm or helpless to care for themselves.

faithful Loyal, trustworthy, constant, devoted, dutiful, reliable, genuine, dependable, honest, upright, honorable, unswerving, unwavering, enduring, unchanging, steady, dedicated, steadfast, sincere, conscientious. *God is faithful; He enables believers to become faithful.*

fame To be well known or popular.

fear (1) To be afraid. (2) To honor and respect.

follow (1) Walk behind. (2) Try to imitate or emulate.

forgiveness Through Christ, our wrongdoings are taken away and forgotten. We forgive others in thanksgiving for God's forgiveness.

fortune Money, wealth, accumulation of material possessions.

fruit (1) The sweet part of a seed-bearing plant. (2) The edible part of a plant. (3) Results that have been produced.

genealogy The record of ancestry and descendents of a family.

God's will What God wants and desires for humankind, which includes living in obedience to God's commands, and above all, it is God's will that all people come to faith in Jesus and be saved.

Gospel (1) One of the first four books of the New Testament. (2) The story of Jesus' birth, life, death, and resurrection. (3) The promise of God in both the Old and New Testaments to forgive our sins and offer eternal salvation through the Messiah—Jesus Christ.

gossip Telling someone's personal or private matters.

grace Receiving kindness you *do not* deserve.

greatness (1) Worldly definition—having the most or best of what is valued. (2) God's definition—serving others in humility and for the glory of God.

greed Selfish desire for more money or possessions than one needs.

hallowed Respected as holy and sacred.

holy Set apart for a sacred purpose; pure, without sin.

holy matrimony A man and woman's pledge of faithfulness before God to fulfill their marriage vows.

honor To show respect to; to give credit to.

hope The hope we have in Christ is the certainty (not just a wish) that our faith is based on. "Now faith is the assurance of things hoped for, the conviction of things not seen" (Hebrews 11:1).

humble (1) Not proud. (2) Submissive.

hymn A song of praise to God.

hypocrite A person who pretends to be something they are not; false appearance.

identity The characteristics by which something is specifically recognized or known.

image God's likeness placed in humans, gifting them with reasoning ability and many other attributes, so they can relate to God and live as caretakers of His world.

imitate Copy the actions or behaviors of someone else.

Immanuel Hebrew for "God with us."

incarnate In the flesh, in human form.

inerrant Never wrong.

inexpressible Beyond description.

influence The act or power of producing an effect on a manner of thinking, decision, course of action, or resulting events.

inherit To receive a gift from the estate of someone who has died. One can inherit money, property, jewelry, or something intangible.

inspired Guided directly by a message from God.

invaluable Priceless.

invocation A prayer asking for help and support at the beginning of a service of worship.

jealousy (1) Fear of losing someone's love or affection. (2) Anger, envy, unhappiness because of what someone else has that you want.

Jesus Greek form of Joshua or Jeshua; "the Lord saves."

Judgment Day Also known as the Last Day, the second coming, Christ's return.

justification What God does *for us* through Jesus. We are rescued by Jesus' death and resurrection.

justified To be declared guiltless or innocent; to be absolved of guilt.

kingdom An area or group of people headed by a king; God's kingdom, or the kingdom of heaven, is made up of all believers.

law Commandment, statute, rule, command, instruction, decree, ordinance, requirement, regulation, mandate, precept, order, direction, summons, obligation.

liturgical arts Various skills, methods, and media used to give glory to God in the construction of a church sanctuary for the purpose of proclaiming a message of God's grace through Christ Jesus.

liturgy The order Christians follow in public worship. Liturgy may be highly formal or more flexible, but it always has some structure that allows worshipers to participate together. A liturgy usually includes hymns, Confession and Absolution, a creed, Bible readings, a sermon, prayers, the Lord's Prayer, Holy Communion, and a benediction.

manifest Apparent, noticeable, straightforward, visible, revealed, easy to see, clear, obvious, unmistakable, proclaimed, shown.

materialism (1) An intense focus on physical things, comforts, or possessions. (2) A false trust that looks to possessions to make one happy or secure.

Means of Grace The tools by which the Holy Spirit gives to individuals the forgiveness Jesus won for all on the cross. The Means of Grace are the Word of the Gospel (both written and spoken) and the Sacraments (Baptism and the Lord's Supper). These means are the only ways God has promised to create and strengthen faith in people's hearts.

medieval A period of many centuries of domination by royalty and clergy in European history.

merciful Characterized by compassion, pity, concern; the willingness to help someone in need, especially an enemy.

mercy *Not* receiving punishment you *do* deserve.

Messiah Hebrew for "anointed."

modest Humble in appearance.

morality Good character/behavior that follows a value system of right and wrong.

Office of the Keys The authority Jesus gave to His Church here on earth to forgive the sins of those who repent and to refuse absolution to the impenitent; congregations call pastors to use the Office of the Keys publically on the congregation's behalf.

opportunity Favorable occasion, a fortunate possibility, or a convenient time.

organization People or groups working together for a united purpose.

Pentecost (1) Old Testament times—a harvest thanksgiving festival held fifty days after Passover. (2) New Testament times—a celebration of the pouring of the Holy Spirit on the Christian Church fifty days after Easter.

perish (1) To die physically (Matthew 8:25). (2) To die spiritually and eternally (John 3:16).

persecution Mistreatment, including verbal and physical assault, of a person or a group because of their beliefs.

petition Request; ask for something.

plainsong A rhythmically free liturgical chant.

pledge A heartfelt, sincere promise or agreement.

preserve Protect; safeguard.

primary source Spoken or written information from a person who actually witnessed or participated in an event.

prophesy To tell what or who is coming.

prophet One who speaks a message from God (can be a prediction or warning or an encouragement).

propitiation The act of gaining or regaining favor or goodwill. Something that gains or regains the favor or goodwill, specifically, an atoning sacrifice.

protestant (1) Broadly—a Christian church denomination not of the Catholic Church or Eastern Orthodox Church. (2) Specifically—a member of any of several church denominations denying the universal authority of the pope and affirming the Reformation principles of justification by faith alone, the priesthood of all believers, and the primacy of the Bible as the only source of revealed truth.

pure Innocent, without guilt, free from impurities.

redeem To buy back or to pay a debt owed by someone else. Jesus came to redeem all people from slavery to sin and death.

He paid the price to set us free not with money but with His own blood.

redeemer Person who buys back.

reflect To mirror the likeness, image, or characteristics of someone else.

Reformation A point in history where God blessed the Church with reformers who bravely proclaimed a return to the pure truth of God's Word, especially in the Gospel of salvation through Christ Jesus.

regeneration Spiritual rebirth, becoming new again.

relationships Your connection to, interactions with, and associations with other people.

rely (1) To be dependent on. (2) To have confidence based on experience.

remember Celebrate, observe a ceremony.

Renaissance An era of great changes in culture and academics led by greater individual independence of thought.

renewal To begin again, restored to a condition that had been lost or damaged.

repentance The change of heart and the renewed trust for God that leads to changed behaviors.

reputation The respect and value in which someone's character is regarded.

restored As Jesus forgives us, we live new lives in repentance and faith.

revere To feel deep respect, honor, and awe.

rival One who attempts to compete to equal or surpass another or pursues the same object or goal.

Sabbath Rest and relief from cares and troubles.

Sacrament A sacred act instituted by God, in which He has joined His Word of promise to a visible element and in which He offers the forgiveness of sins earned by Christ's death and resurrection. The two Sacraments are Holy Baptism and the Lord's Supper.

sacred Honored as holy and dedicated to God.

sacrifice To give up something you value very much.

saints Christian believers; people whom God has made holy through the forgiveness of Christ Jesus. A saint can be either a Christian who is alive on earth or one who is already in heaven.

sanctification What God does *in us* through the Holy Spirit. We are set free by the empowering gifts of the Spirit. The ongoing work of the Holy Spirit to keep us in faith, strengthen that faith, and live a life of faith; the Holy Spirit sanctifies us as He works through the Means of Grace, which are God's Word and the Sacraments of Holy Baptism and the Lord's Supper.

sanctuary (1) A consecrated place of safety, peace, and meditation. (2) A place set aside where we worship God—God's house.

Satan The chief of the fallen angels; created holy by God, Satan later rebelled against Him. The name "Satan" means "adversary." He is the enemy of God and God's people.

seraphim Angels of a specific rank or grouping; in Hebrew, the word means "the burning ones," perhaps because the seraphim burn with love for God and zeal to serve Him. These are sometimes described as having six wings.

slander To spread malicious or false rumors.

soul The breath of life from God that gives the rational immortal spirit by which humans are distinguished from animals.

spontaneous Automatic, free, impromptu, improvised, natural, uncontrived, unplanned, unpremeditated, voluntary.

state of:

(1) **humiliation** Christ did not always or fully use His divine powers (Philippians 2:5–8).

(2) **exaltation** Christ now fully and always uses His divine powers (Philippians 2:9–11).

stewardship Being responsible for what someone has entrusted to your care; managing someone else's property or possessions wisely and well.

suicide Taking one's own life.

swear To call on God's name to witness to the truth of what you say, asking Him to punish you if you break your promise.

synagogue The house of worship and instruction for a Jewish congregation.

testament A declaration; a covenant.

treasurer Someone in charge of the receipt, care, and disbursement of something valuable; trustee; steward.

Trinity The one true God in three persons: Father, Son, and Holy Spirit; Three in One; also called the triune God.

trust (1) To have confidence in. (2) To be certain.

vocation A person's career, occupation, role, or calling.

vow A solemn promise, made before God and witnesses; to make a personal commitment regarding actions in the future.

walk (1) Take steps. (2) Behave or live in a certain way.

will Desire; what is wanted. Seeking God's will means looking to do what God wants to be done.

witness Telling others what you know is true.

worthy Deserving, honorable, upright, of value.

SECTION 1

THE TEN COMMANDMENTS

The First Commandment:

You shall have no other gods

What does this mean? We should fear, love, and trust in God above all things.

The Second Commandment:

You shall not misuse the name of the Lord your God.

What does this mean? We should fear and love God so that we do not curse, swear, use satanic arts, lie, or deceive by His name, but call upon it in every trouble, pray, praise, and give thanks.

The Third Commandment:

Remember the Sabbath day by keeping it holy.

What does this mean? We should fear and love God so that we do not despise preaching and His Word, but hold it sacred and gladly hear and learn it.

The Fourth Commandment:

Honor your father and your mother.

What does this mean? We should fear and love God so that we do not despise or anger our parents and other authorities, but honor them, serve and obey them, love and cherish them.

The Fifth Commandment:

You shall not murder.

What does this mean? We should fear and love God so that we do not hurt or harm our neighbor in his body, but help and support him in every physical need.

The Sixth Commandment:

You shall not commit adultery.

What does this mean? We should fear and love God so that we lead a sexually pure and decent life in what we say and do, and husband and wife love and honor each other.

The Seventh Commandment:

You shall not steal.

What does this mean? We should fear and love God so that we do not take our neighbor's money or possessions, or get them in any dishonest way, but help him to improve and protect his possessions and income.

The Eighth Commandment:

You shall not give false testimony against your neighbor.

What does this mean? We should fear and love God so that we do not tell lies about our neighbor, betray him, slander him, or hurt his reputation, but defend him, speak well of him, and explain everything in the kindest way.

The Ninth Commandment:

You shall not covet your neighbor's house.

What does this mean? We should fear and love God so that we do not scheme to get our neighbor's inheritance or house, or get it in a way which only appears right, but help and be of service to him in keeping it.

The Tenth Commandment:

You shall not covet your neighbor's wife,
or his manservant or maidservant, his ox or donkey,
or anything that belongs to your neighbor.

What does this mean? We should fear and love God so that we do not entice or force away our neighbor's wife, workers, or animals, or turn them against him, but urge them to stay and do their duty.

The Close of the Commandments:

What does does God say about all these commandments? He says, "I, the Lord your God, am a jealous God, punishing the children for the sin of the fathers to the third and fourth generation of those who hate Me, but showing love to a thousand generations of those who love Me and keep My commandments." (Exodus 20:5–6)

What does this mean? God threatens to punish all who break these commandments. Therefore, we should fear His wrath and not do anything against them. But He promises grace and every blessing to all who keep these commandments. Therefore, we should also love and trust in Him and gladly do what He commands.

THE CREED

The First Article (Creation)

I believe in God, the Father Almighty, Maker of heaven and earth.

What does this mean? I believe that God has made me and all creatures; that He has given me my body and soul, eyes, ears, and all my members, my reason and all my senses, and still takes care of them.

He also gives me clothing and shoes, food and drink, house and home, wife and children, land, animals, and all I have. He richly and daily provides me with all that I need to support this body and life.

He defends me against all danger and guards and protects me from all evil.

All this He does only out of fatherly, divine goodness and mercy, without any merit or worthiness in me. For all this it is my duty to thank and praise, serve and obey Him.

This is most certainly true.

The Second Article (Redemption)

And in Jesus Christ, His only Son, our Lord, who was conceived by the Holy Spirit, born of the Virgin Mary, suffered under Pontius Pilate, was crucified, died and was buried. He descended into hell. The third day He rose again from the dead. He ascended into heaven and sits at the right hand of God, the Father Almighty. From thence He will come to judge the living and the dead.

What does this mean? I believe that Jesus Christ, true God, begotten of the Father from eternity, and also true man, born of the Virgin Mary, is my Lord, who has redeemed me, a lost and condemned person, purchased and won me from all sins, from death, and from the power of the devil; not with gold or silver, but with His holy, precious blood and with His innocent suffering and death, that I may be His own and live under Him in His kingdom and serve Him in everlasting righteousness, innocence, and blessedness, just as He is risen from the dead, lives and reigns to all eternity.

This is most certainly true.

The Third Article *(Sanctification)*

I believe in the Holy Spirit, the holy Christian church, the communion of saints, the forgiveness of sins, the resurrection of the body, and the life everlasting. Amen.

What does this mean? I believe that I cannot by my own reason or strength believe in Jesus Christ, my Lord, or come to Him; but the Holy Spirit has called me by the Gospel, enlightened me with His gifts, sanctified and kept me in the true faith.

In the same way He calls, gathers, enlightens, and sanctifies the whole Christian church on earth, and keeps it with Jesus Christ in the one true faith.

In this Christian church He daily and richly forgives all my sins and the sins of all believers.

On the Last Day He will raise me and all the dead, and give eternal life to me and all believers in Christ.

This is most certainly true.

THE LORD'S PRAYER

The Introduction: Our Father who art in heaven.

What does this mean? With these words God tenderly invites us to believe that He is our true Father and that we are His true children, so that with all boldness and confidence we may ask Him as dear children ask their dear father.

The First Petition: Hallowed be Thy name.

What does this mean? God's name is certainly holy in itself, but we pray in this petition that it may be kept holy among us also.
How is God's name kept holy? God's name is kept holy when the Word of God is taught in its truth and purity, and we, as the children of God, also lead holy lives according to it. Help us to do this, dear Father in heaven! But anyone who teaches or lives contrary to God's Word profanes the name of God among us. Protect us from this, heavenly Father!

The Second Petition: Thy kingdom come.

What does this mean? The kingdom of God certainly comes by itself without our prayer, but we pray in this petition that it may come to us also.
How does God's kingdom come? God's kingdom comes when our heavenly Father gives us His Holy Spirit, so that by His grace we believe His holy Word and lead godly lives here in time and there in eternity.

The Third Petition: Thy will be done on earth as it is in heaven.

What does this mean? The good and gracious will of God is done even without our prayer, but we pray in this petition that it may be done among us also.
How is God's will done? God's will is done when He breaks and hinders every evil plan and purpose of the devil, the world, and our sinful nature, which do not want us to hallow God's name or let His kingdom come; and when He strengthens and keeps us firm in His Word and faith until we die. This is His good and gracious will.

The Fourth Petition: Give us this day our daily bread.

What does this mean? God certainly gives daily bread to everyone without our prayers, even to all evil people, but we pray in this petition that God would lead us to realize this and to receive our daily bread with thanksgiving.

What is meant by daily bread? Daily bread includes everything that has to do with the support and needs of the body, such as food, drink, clothing, shoes, house, home, land, animals, money, goods, a devout husband or wife, devout children, devout workers, devout and faithful rulers, good government, good weather, peace, health, self-control, good reputation, good friends, faithful neighbors, and the like.

The Fifth Petition: And forgive us our trespasses as we forgive those who trespass against us.

What does this mean? We pray in this petition that our Father in heaven would not look at our sins, or deny our prayer because of them. We are neither worthy of the things for which we pray, nor have we deserved them, but we ask that He would give them all to us by grace, for we daily sin much and surely deserve nothing but punishment. So we too will sincerely forgive and gladly do good to those who sin against us.

The Sixth Petition: And lead us not into temptation.

What does this mean? God tempts no one. We pray in this petition that God would guard and keep us so that the devil, the world, and our sinful nature may not deceive us or mislead us into false belief, despair, and other great shame and vice. Although we are attacked by these things, we pray that we may finally overcome them and win the victory.

The Seventh Petition: But deliver us from evil.

What does this mean? We pray in this petition, in summary, that our Father in heaven would rescue us from every evil of body and soul, possessions and reputation, and finally, when our last hour comes, give us a blessed end, and graciously take us from this valley of sorrow to Himself in heaven.

The Conclusion: For Thine is the kingdom and the power and the glory forever and ever. Amen.

What does this mean? This means that I should be certain that these petitions are pleasing to our Father in heaven, and are heard by Him; for He Himself has commanded us to pray in this way and has promised to hear us. Amen, amen means "yes, yes, it shall be so."

THE SACRAMENT OF HOLY BAPTISM

FIRST

What is Baptism? Baptism is not just plain water, but it is the water included in God's command and combined with God's word.

Which is that word of God? Christ our Lord says in the last chapter of Matthew: "Therefore go and make disciples of all nations, baptizing them in the name of the Father and of the Son and of the Holy Spirit." (Matthew 28:19)

SECOND

What benefits does Baptism give? It works forgiveness of sins, rescues from death and the devil, and gives eternal salvation to all who believe this, as the words and promises of God declare.

Which are these words and promises of God? Christ our Lord says in the last chapter of Mark: "Whoever believes and is baptized will be saved, but whoever does not believe will be condemned." (Mark 16:16)

THIRD

How can water do such great things? Certainly not just water, but the word of God in and with the water does these things, along with the faith which trusts this word of God in the water. For without God's word the water is plain water and no Baptism. But with the word of God it is a Baptism, that is, a life-giving water, rich in grace, and a washing of the new birth in the Holy Spirit, as St. Paul says in Titus, chapter three: "He saved us through the washing of rebirth and renewal by the Holy Spirit, whom He poured out on us generously through Jesus Christ our Savior, so that, having been justified by His grace, we might become heirs having the hope of eternal life. This is a trustworthy saying." (Titus 3:5–8)

FOURTH

What does such baptizing with water indicate? It indicates that the Old Adam in us should by daily contrition and repentance be drowned and die with all sins and evil desires, and that a new man should daily emerge and arise to live before God in righteousness and purity forever.

Where is this written? St. Paul writes in Romans chapter six: "We were therefore buried with Him through baptism into death in order that, just as Christ was raised from the dead through the glory of the Father, we too may live a new life." (Romans 6:4)

CONFESSION

What is Confession? Confession has two parts. First, that we confess our sins, and second, that we receive absolution, that is, forgiveness, from the pastor as from God Himself, not doubting, but firmly believing that by it our sins are forgiven before God in heaven.

What sins should we confess? Before God we should plead guilty of all sins, even those we are not aware of, as we do in the Lord's Prayer; but before the pastor we should confess only those sins which we know and feel in our hearts.

Which are these? Consider your place in life according to the Ten Commandments: Are you a father, mother, son, daughter, husband, wife, or worker? Have you been disobedient, unfaithful, or lazy? Have you been hot-tempered, rude, or quarrelsome? Have you hurt someone by your words or deeds? Have you stolen, been negligent, wasted anything, or done any harm?

What is the Office of the Keys? The Office of the Keys is that special authority which Christ has given to His church on earth to forgive the sins of repentant sinners, but to withhold forgiveness from the unrepentant as long as they do not repent.

Where is this written? This is what St. John the Evangelist writes in chapter twenty: The Lord Jesus breathed on His disciples and said, "Receive the Holy Spirit. If you forgive anyone his sins, they are forgiven; if you do not forgive them, they are not forgiven." (John 20:22–23)

What do you believe according to these words? I believe that when the called ministers of Christ deal with us by His divine command, in particular when they exclude openly unrepentant sinners from the Christian congregation and absolve those who repent of their sins and want to do better, this is just as valid and certain, even in heaven, as if Christ our dear Lord dealt with us Himself.

THE SACRAMENT OF THE ALTAR

What is the Sacrament of the Altar? It is the true body and blood of our Lord Jesus Christ under the bread and wine, instituted by Christ Himself for us Christians to eat and to drink.

Where is this written? The holy Evangelists Matthew, Mark, Luke, and St. Paul write: Our Lord Jesus Christ, on the night when He was betrayed, took bread, and when He had given thanks, He broke it and gave it to the disciples and said: "Take, eat; this is My body, which is given for you. This do in remembrance of Me." In the same way also He took the cup after supper, and when He had given thanks, He gave it to them, saying, "Drink of it, all of you; this cup is the new testament in My blood, which is shed for you for the forgiveness of sins. This do, as often as you drink it, in remembrance of Me."

What is the benefit of this eating and drinking? These words, "Given and shed for you for the forgiveness of sins," show us that in the Sacrament forgiveness of sins, life, and salvation are given us through these words. For where there is forgiveness of sins, there is also life and salvation.

How can bodily eating and drinking do such great things? Certainly not just eating and drinking do these things, but the words written here: "Given and shed for you for the forgiveness of sins." These words, along with the bodily eating and drinking, are the main thing in the Sacrament. Whoever believes these words has exactly what they say: "forgiveness of sins."

Who receives this sacrament worthily? Fasting and bodily preparation are certainly fine outward training. But that person is truly worthy and well prepared who has faith in these words: "Given and shed for you for the forgiveness of sins." But anyone who does not believe these words or doubts them is unworthy and unprepared, for the words "for you" require all hearts to believe.

DAILY PRAYERS

Morning Prayer

*In the morning when you get up, make the sign of the holy cross and say:
In the name of the Father and of the Son and of the Holy Spirit. Amen.*

I thank You, my heavenly Father, through Jesus Christ, Your dear Son, that You have kept me this night from all harm and danger; and I pray that You would keep me this day also from sin and every evil, that all my doings and life may please You. For into Your hands I commend myself, my body and soul, and all things. Let Your holy angel be with me, that the evil foe may have no power over me. Amen.

Evening Prayer

*In the evening when you go to bed, make the sign of the holy cross and say:
In the name of the Father and of the Son and of the Holy Spirit. Amen.*

I thank You, my heavenly Father, through Jesus Christ, Your dear Son, that You have graciously kept me this day; and I pray that You would forgive me all my sins where I have done wrong, and graciously keep me this night. For into Your hands I commend myself, my body and soul, and all things. Let Your holy angel be with me, that the evil foe may have no power over me. Amen.

Asking a Blessing

The eyes of all look to You, [O Lord,] and You give them their food at the proper time. You open Your hand and satisfy the desires of every living thing. (Psalm 145:15–16)

Returning Thanks

Give thanks to the Lord, for He is good. His love endures forever. [He] gives food to every creature. He provides food for the cattle and for the young ravens when they call. His pleasure is not in the strength of the horse, nor His delight in the legs of a man; the Lord delights in those who fear Him, who put their hope in His unfailing love. (Psalm 136:1, 25; 147:9–11)

We thank You, Lord God, heavenly Father, for all Your benefits, through Jesus Christ, our Lord, who lives and reigns with You and the Holy Spirit forever and ever. Amen.

SECTION 3

TABLE OF DUTIES

Certain passages of Scripture for various holy orders and positions, admonishing them about their duties and responsibilities

To Bishops, Pastors, and Preachers

The overseer must be above reproach, the husband of but one wife, temperate, self-controlled, respectable, hospitable, able to teach, not given to drunkenness, not violent but gentle, not quarrelsome, not a lover of money. He must manage his own family well and see that his children obey him with proper respect. (1 Timothy 3:2–4)

He must not be a recent convert, or he may become conceited and fall under the same judgment as the devil. (1 Timothy 3:6)

He must hold firmly to the trustworthy message as it has been taught, so that he can encourage others by sound doctrine and refute those who oppose it. (Titus 1:9)

What the Hearers Owe Their Pastors

The Lord has commanded that those who preach the gospel should receive their living from the gospel. (1 Corinthians 9:14)

Anyone who receives instruction in the word must share all good things with his instructor. Do not be deceived: God cannot be mocked. A man reaps what he sows. (Galatians 6:6–7)

The elders who direct the affairs of the church well are worthy of double honor, especially those whose work is preaching and teaching. For the Scripture says, "Do not muzzle the ox while it is treading out the grain," and "The worker deserves his wages." (1 Timothy 5:17–18)

We ask you, brothers, to respect those who work hard among you, who are over you in the Lord and who admonish you. Hold them in the highest regard in love because of their work. Live in peace with each other. (1 Thessalonians 5:12–13)

Obey your leaders and submit to their authority. They keep watch over you as men who must give an account. Obey them so that their work will be a joy, not a burden, for that would be of no advantage to you. (Hebrews 13:17)

Of Civil Government

Everyone must submit himself to the governing authorities, for there is no authority except that which God has established. The authorities that exist have been established by God. Consequently, he who rebels against the authority is rebelling against what God has instituted, and those who do so will bring judgment on themselves. For rulers hold no terror for those who do right, but for those who do wrong. Do you want to be free from fear of the one in authority? Then do what is right and he will commend you. For he is God's servant to do you good. But if you do wrong, be afraid, for he does not bear the sword for nothing. He is God's servant, an agent of wrath to bring punishment on the wrongdoer. (Romans 13:1–4)

Of Citizens

Give to Caesar what is Caesar's, and to God what is God's. (Matthew 22:21)

It is necessary to submit to the authorities, not only because of possible punishment but also because of conscience. This is also why you pay taxes, for the authorities are God's servants, who give their full time to governing. Give everyone what you owe him: If you owe taxes, pay taxes; if revenue, then revenue; if respect, then respect; if honor, then honor. (Romans 13:5–7)

I urge, then, first of all, that requests, prayers, intercession and thanksgiving be made for everyone—for kings and all those in authority, that we may live peaceful and quiet lives in all godliness and holiness. This is good, and pleases God our Savior. (1 Timothy 2:1–3)

Remind the people to be subject to rulers and authorities, to be obedient, to be ready to do whatever is good. (Titus 3:1)

Submit yourselves for the Lord's sake to every authority instituted among men: whether to the king, as the supreme authority, or to governors, who are sent by him to punish those who do wrong and to commend those who do right. (1 Peter 2:13–14)

To Husbands

Husbands, in the same way be considerate as you live with your wives, and treat them with respect as the weaker partner and as heirs with you of the gracious gift of life, so that nothing will hinder your prayers. (1 Peter 3:7)

Husbands, love your wives and do not be harsh with them. (Colossians 3:19)

To Wives

Wives, submit to your husbands as to the Lord. (Ephesians 5:22)
They were submissive to their own husbands, like Sarah, who obeyed
Abraham and called him her master. You are her daughters if you do what
is right and do not give way to fear. (1 Peter 3:5–6)

To Parents

Fathers, do not exasperate your children; instead, bring them up in the
training and instruction of the Lord. (Ephesians 6:4)

To Children

Children, obey your parents in the Lord, for this is right. "Honor your
father and your mother"—which is the first commandment with a
promise—"that it may go well with you and that you may enjoy long life on
the earth." (Ephesians 6:1–3)

To Workers of All Kinds

Slaves, obey your earthly masters with respect and fear, and with
sincerity of heart, just as you would obey Christ. Obey them not only
to win their favor when their eye is on you, but like slaves of Christ,
doing the will of God from your heart. Serve wholeheartedly, as if you
were serving the Lord, not men, because you know that the Lord will
reward everyone for whatever good he does, whether he is slave or free.
(Ephesians 6:5–8)

To Employers and Supervisors

Masters, treat your slaves in the same way. Do not threaten them, since
you know that He who is both their Master and yours is in heaven, and
there is no favoritism with Him. (Ephesians 6:9)

To Youth

Young men, in the same way be submissive to those who are older. All of
you, clothe yourselves with humility toward one another, because, "God
opposes the proud but gives grace to the humble." Humble yourselves,
therefore, under God's mighty hand, that He may lift you up in due time.
(1 Peter 5:5–6)

To Widows

The widow who is really in need and left all alone puts her hope in God and continues night and day to pray and to ask God for help. But the widow who lives for pleasure is dead even while she lives. (1 Timothy 5:5–6)

To Everyone

The commandments . . . are summed up in this one rule: "Love your neighbor as yourself." (Romans 13:9)

I urge . . . that requests, prayers, intercession and thanksgiving be made for everyone. (1 Timothy 2:1)

CHRISTIAN QUESTIONS WITH THEIR ANSWERS

Prepared by Dr. Martin Luther for those who intend to go to the Sacrament. After confession and instruction in the Ten Commandments, the Creed, the Lord's Prayer, and the Sacraments of Baptism and the Lord's Supper, the pastor may ask, or Christians may ask themselves these questions:

1. Do you believe that you are a sinner?

    Yes, I believe it. I am a sinner.

2. How do you know this?

    From the Ten Commandments, which I have not kept.

3. Are you sorry for your sins?

    Yes, I am sorry that I have sinned against God.

4. What have you deserved from God because of your sins?

    His wrath and displeasure, temporal death, and eternal damnation. See Romans 6:21, 23.

5. Do you hope to be saved?

    Yes, that is my hope.

6. In whom then do you trust?

    In my dear Lord Jesus Christ.

7. Who is Christ?

    The Son of God, true God and man.

8. How many Gods are there?

    Only one, but there are three persons: Father, Son, and Holy Spirit.

9. What has Christ done for you that you trust in Him?

    He died for me and shed His blood for me on the cross for the forgiveness of sins.

10. Did the Father also die for you?

    He did not. The Father is God only, as is the Holy Spirit; but the Son is both true God and true man. He died for me and shed His blood for me.

11. How do you know this?

    From the Holy Gospel, from the words instituting the Sacrament, and by His body and blood given me as a pledge in the Sacrament.

12. What are the Words of Institution?

    Our Lord Jesus Christ, on the night when He was betrayed, took bread, and when He had given thanks, He broke it and gave it to the disciples and said: "Take, eat; this is My body, which is given for you. This do in remembrance of Me." In the same way also He took the cup after supper, and when He had given thanks, He gave it to them, saying: "Drink of it, all of you; this cup is the new testament in My blood, which is shed for you for the forgiveness of sins. This do, as often as you drink it, in remembrance of Me."

13. Do you believe, then, that the true body and blood of Christ are in the Sacrament?

> Yes, I believe it.

14. What convinces you to believe this?

> The word of Christ: Take, eat, this is My body; drink of it, all of you, this is My blood.

15. What should we do when we eat His body and drink His blood, and in this way receive His pledge?

> We should remember and proclaim His death and the shedding of His blood, as He taught us: This do, as often as you drink it, in remembrance of Me.

16. Why should we remember and proclaim His death?

> First, so that we may learn to believe that no creature could make satisfaction for our sins. Only Christ, true God and man, could do that. Second, so we may learn to be horrified by our sins, and to regard them as very serious. Third, so we may find joy and comfort in Christ alone, and through faith in Him be saved.

17. What motivated Christ to die and make full payment for your sins?

> His great love for His Father and for me and other sinners, as it is written in John 14; Romans 5; Galatians 2; and Ephesians 5.

18. Finally, why do you wish to go to the Sacrament?

> That I may learn to believe that Christ, out of great love, died for my sin, and also learn from Him to love God and my neighbor.

19. What should admonish and encourage a Christian to receive the Sacrament frequently?

> First, both the command and the promise of Christ the Lord. Second, his own pressing need, because of which the command, encouragement, and promise are given.

20. But what should you do if you are not aware of this need and have no hunger and thirst for the Sacrament?

> To such a person no better advice can be given than this: first, he should touch his body to see if he still has flesh and blood. Then he should believe what the Scriptures say of it in Galatians 5 and Romans 7. Second, he should look around to see whether he is still in the world, and remember that there will be no lack of sin and trouble, as the Scriptures say in John 15–16 and in 1 John 2 and 5. Third, he will certainly have the devil also around him, who with his lying and murdering day and night will let him have no peace, within or without, as the Scriptures picture him in John 8 and 16; 1 Peter 5; Ephesians 6; and 2 Timothy 2.

Table of Contents